IPHIGENIA AND THE FURIES
(On Taurian Land).

ANTIGONE:方

IPHIGENIA AND THE FURIES
(On Taurian Land)

ANTIGONE: 方

HO KA KEI

(Jeff Ho)

PLAYWRIGHTS CANADA PRESS
TORONTO

For professional or amateur production rights, please contact:
Ian Arnold, Catalyst TCM Inc.
15 Old Primrose Lane, Toronto, ON M5A 4T1
(416) 568-8673 | ian@catalysttcm.com

LIBRARY AND ARCHIVES CANADA CATALOGUING IN PUBLICATION
Title: Iphigenia and the furies (on Taurian land) ; & Antigone : fang / Ho Ka Kei.
Other titles: Plays. Selections | Antigone
Names: Ho, Jeff, author. | Container of (work): Ho, Jeff. Iphigenia and the furies
    (on Taurian land) | Container of (work): Ho, Jeff. Antigone. | adaptation of (work):
    Euripides. Iphigenia in Tauris. | adaptation of (work): Sophocles. Antigone.
Description: Two plays.
Identifiers: Canadiana (print) 20220133301 | Canadiana (ebook) 20220133484
    | ISBN 9780369103024 (softcover) | ISBN 9780369103031 (PDF)
    | ISBN 9780369103048 (HTML)
Classification: LCC PS8615.O155 A6 2022 | DDC C812/.6—dc23

Playwrights Canada Press operates on land which is the ancestral home of the
Anishinaabe Nations (Ojibwe / Chippewa, Odawa, Potawatomi, Algonquin, Saulteaux,
Nipissing, and Mississauga), the Wendat, and the members of the Haudenosaunee
Confederacy (Mohawk, Oneida, Onondaga, Cayuga, Seneca, and Tuscarora), as well
as Metis and Inuit peoples. It always was and always will be Indigenous land.

We acknowledge the financial support of the Canada Council for the Arts, the Ontario
Arts Council (OAC), Ontario Creates, and the Government of Canada for our pub-
lishing activities.

Canada Council   Conseil des arts
for the Arts   du Canada

ONTARIO ARTS COUNCIL
CONSEIL DES ARTS DE L'ONTARIO
an Ontario government agency
un organisme du gouvernement de l'Ontario

Canadä

ONTARIO | ONTARIO
CREATES | CRÉATIF

For all who fight to remember truth.

FOREWORD

BY JONATHAN SEINEN

Ho Ka Kei's *Antigone: 方* and *Iphigenia and the Furies (On Taurian Land)* are necessary adaptations of Greek texts by Sophocles and Euripides respectively. Both contain undeniable dramatic potency, which Ho embraces wholeheartedly, but he plants them firmly in our times, reimagining these two plays through an unflinchingly contemporary lens.

Antigone is a text that survives to this day via multiple, and many recent, adaptations: Canadian poet Anne Carson's two translations, including a Hegel-quoting graphic novel edition; Slovenian philosopher Slavoj Žižek's "ethico-political exercise"* with three different endings; Québécoise director Sophie Deraspe's film that locates the drama amongst a refugee family in Montreal in which the hero impersonates her brother to free him from prison; and *Antigone in Ferguson*, created by the American company Theater of War Productions with a choir of community members from St. Louis, Missouri, in response to the 2014 police killing of Michael Brown. The play exists as a call for justice, and in each new version of this ancient Greek tragedy, an audience is called to meet themselves in the moment in which they live.

Ho contributes his own significant intervention to this tradition, reframing a story that "swell[s] back to life generation after generation" by transporting *Antigone*—subtitled " 方," the Kangxi radical that translates to "the square"—to an unnamed but recognizable city where protests have erupted and threaten the dominant power structure. Allusions to the 2014 Hong Kong Umbrella Movement and the 1989 Beijing Tiananmen Square protest and massacre combine and, for Ho, a Hong Kong native,

---

* Žižek, Slavoj. *Antigone*. Bloomsbury, 1996, p. xxv.

this unified setting is a lived reality; he is a playwright who recognizes he can, and perhaps must, speak for those who are silenced. Ho gives voice to those who "vibrate between the law and [their] lives," highlighting the interpersonal level at which political events shake and shape us, such as the interfamilial battles born out of the Cultural Revolution.

While *Antigone* is widely known, *Iphigenia Among the Taurians* (as Carson's translation would have it) is less so. I first approached Ho to play the role of Pylades in an independent production I was imagining for Saga Collectif that featured Virgilia Griffith and Thomas Antony Olajide as the titular character and her brother. Ho countered by suggesting he write an original adaptation, and I jumped at the offer.

While we wanted to hold on to the original's genre-bending tendencies and grandeur of scale and stakes, our collaboration gave Ho's imagination free rein. Ho follows the plot as far as the middle of the play, right up to Aristotle's favourite recognition scene, of which he writes, "the best is that which arises from the incidents themselves, where the startling discovery is made by natural means . . . It was natural that Iphigenia should wish to dispense a letter."* Ho centres this *anagnorisis*—initiated by Pylades delivering the letter to Orestes in Iphigenia's presence—in his adaptation, but after that, he goes his own way.

For that first production, we entered rehearsals with a script still in flux, a brave acting company on board for the ride, and a dedicated creative team. It was a quick but rich process, full of trial and error, conversation and accountability, integrating elements from each of our stories into the story we were telling. I remember clearly one day when actor Augusto Bitter (who played Pylades) brought in queer Chicana feminist icon Gloria Anzaldúa's book *Borderlands/La Frontera: The New Mestiza* and asked Griffith to read an excerpt:

> But it is not enough to stand on the opposite river bank, shout-
> ing questions, challenging patriarchal, white conventions
> . . . The counterstance refutes the dominant culture's views
> and beliefs, and, for this, it is proudly defiant . . . it's a step
> towards liberation from the cultural domination. But it is not

---

* Aristotle. *Aristotle's Poetics*. Translated by S.H. Butcher, Hill and Wang, 1961, p. 86.

a way of life. At some point, on our way to a new conscious-
ness, we will have to leave the opposite bank, the split between
the two mortal combatants somehow healed so that we are
on both shores at once and, at once, see through serpent and
eagle eyes . . . The possibilities are numerous once we decide
to act and not react.*

This is the work Ho is engaged in: demonstrating the metaphoric
possibilities of the theatre. Refusing one-to-one analogies and refuting
fixed meaning, Ho's counterstance is to demand equal time with these
"canonical" texts of Western culture, keeping their dramatic power alive
but interrogating the illusions they've upheld to propose a different way
forward. Our theatre is richer for it.

*Jonathan Seinen is a founding member of Saga Collectif and Boys
in Chairs Collective, co-artistic producer of Architect Theatre, and
a former artistic associate with lemonTree creations. In addition
to directing* Black Boys, *he directed* Iphigenia and the Furies
(On Taurian Land), *which was nominated for seven Dora Mavor
Moore Awards, including Outstanding Direction, co-created and
performed in* Highway 63: The Fort Mac Show *and* Like There's
No Tomorrow, *and was Assistant Director for* Timon of Athens *at
the Stratford Festival. He co-created* Charisma Furs *with Mx. Sly,
which was published by Playwrights Canada Press in Q2Q: Queer
Canadian Performance Texts. A graduate of the National Theatre
School of Canada, he earned his* M.F.A. *in Theatre Directing at
Columbia University in New York City, where he directed* Cabaret,
Our Town, *and* The Seagull, *and was Assistant Director to Anne
Bogart on* Tristan Und Isolde *at the Croatian National Theatre
in Rijeka. He is a winner of the Canada Council for the Arts John
Hirsch Prize, and is currently Assistant Professor at* SUNY *Buffalo
State College in Buffalo, New York.*

---

* Anzaldúa, Gloria. *Borderlands/La Frontera: The New Mestiza*. Auntie Luti Books,
1987, pp. 78–79.

IPHIGENIA AND THE FURIES

(On Taurian Land)

Iphigenia and the Furies (On Taurian Land) was first produced by Saga Collectif at the Aki Studio Theatre, Daniels Spectrum, Toronto, from January 6 to 20, 2019, with the following cast and creative team:

Pylades: Augusto Bitter
Iphigenia: Virgilia Griffith
Chorus: PJ Prudat
Orestes: Thomas Antony Olajide

Director: Jonathan Seinen
Dramaturg: Charlotte Corbeil-Coleman
Set and Costume Design: Christine Urquhart
Sound Design and Music: Heidi Chan
Lighting Design: Jareth Li
Stage Manager: Farnoosh Talebpour
Assistant Director: Jay Northcott
Producer: Indrit Kasapi
Associate Producer: Kourtney Jackson
Production Manager and Technical Director: Giuseppe Condello

CHARACTERS

Iphigenia
Orestes
Pylades
Chorus

NOTES ON CASTING

The play was written and produced within a Canadian context, with IBPOC actors in mind, and with an Indigenous chorus member.

When casting for this play, please use due diligence and care in reflecting the conversations around indigeneity, race, colonialism, and cycles of trauma within your own communities. The cast must reflect this conversation within your own political and geographical contexts.

NOTES ON TEXT

A forward slash (/) is an interruption, and marks when characters cut each other off.

SETTING

Tauros. The entrance to the Temple of Artemis.

All props and set pieces are to be shaped entirely of white paper.

PROLOGUE.

CHORUS enters and regards the playing space,
The audience,
The ceiling,
The floor,
The walls.
Finds centre.

And wherever we are,
Whoever we are,
We have to know, respect, and honour
The losses, sacrifices, traumas, scars, and souls
That have come before, recorded or unrecorded,
Of this land.

We must pay respect to our ancestors,
And even across cultures
We have to face facts—of the colonial terrors perpetuated
And that continue to be perpetuated
On this land.

CHORUS, whoever you may be,
Acknowledges all that has come before
In this very space,
And places a palm on the ground,
Connecting with the land
For and with us all.

CHORUS takes a moment
And leaves the playing space.

SCENE 1.

> IPHIGENIA *enters,*
> *Passing through the paper temple.*
> *Maybe it crumples, withers, or wrinkles as she passes.*
> *She looks at us.*

IPHIGENIA
I was a princess.
Was.
Now, a priestess.
Of what?
You tell me.
What does this altar look like?
Who is it for?
Why do they, the ones above,
Require such downfall,
Such an outpour of
RED
To be happy?

To ... be ... happy.
Look at me.

I was a princess.
Of the Atreus house.
No more.
Should be dead, technically,
But hey ...
Miracles ...

You know my pa?
Well you should.

The king with the raging unstoppable hard-on for war, war, and
War.
Agamemnon.
Son of Atreus, brother to Menelaus.
He wanted me dead.
Asked if I could kindly pass away
For his safe passage across the sea,
To rescue my aunt, HELEN.

First thing I asked was:
"Um. Why?"

Daddy Aggy goes:
"Cuz Artemis said it's the only way to cross the sea."

"Well, all right,
If Artemis says so then
OFF WITH MY HEAD."

Mom . . . Clytemnestra . . . I call her Clem,
She protested,
She LOVED me.
She wanted me alive.
(Didn't think to ask what *I* wanted.)

So they fought and fought, and finally I said,
"Oh gosh,
Stop bickering already.
Fine, I'll die!
I'll be your pig for slaughter.
Remember me when you sail across the ocean, my
Neck slit,
Throat cut,
Or whatever goddamn death you wanna gift me."

Clem was astonished.
Weeping, going all like,
"Daughter, daughter
Don't."

And I said:
"What?
It's just life,
That's all I'm leaving behind."

And they carried me to Aulis,
Daddy Aggy, Uncle Menelaus, and their thousand ships of Greeks
Ready to set sail for Troy,
All just waiting for my life to end,
So that Helen's could begin again.

Something was done to her.
I dunno . . .
Enough for a thousand ships to set sail for revenge.

Anyway,
Didn't work,
Still alive,
Ta da.

    Beat.

On the day I was supposed t'die,
They lift me up the altar of Aulis,
Thousands of eyes on me,
Thumbs twiddling,
A few yawns here and there.

They take the sickle,
Lift it above my neck . . .

Annnnnnnnnnnd,

Artemis pulls a fuck you on them all,
Whisks me away,
Up up up into the clouds,
Leaves a pig in my place at the altar.
Oink.

So I'm, like, flying through the clouds,
Artemis's fingers latched onto my shoulders,
And I'm all like,
"Let me go! Where are you flying me!?"

Drops me off *here.*

With the Taurians . . .
We used to call them the "barbarians."
Our textbooks called them
Tribal.
All those names we use
To
Strip humans from being humans.

The Taurians have a king.
Thoas.
He's my boss.

The Taurians worship Artemis,
(God knows why).
This is her temple.
I am her priestess,
Her priestess of bloodletting.

You see,
The Taurians have a law.

We sacrifice any foreign man that comes to their lands,
For Artemis's blessing.

I say we because I start the ritual,
Then the sisters do the killing.

I am trapped in a cycle of sacrifice.
Having been spared from one,
I now inflict it as a daily chore.

Now, my life is entirely devoted to dishing death,
And my only mercy is found in dreams.

    Beat.

Wanna hear one?

    Beat.

You have no choice,
This is my story.
You're here for me.

    Beat.

Last night, I dreamt that
I was back home in Argos:

I'm asleep.
The earth shakes, waking me.
I scream, run outside.
I watch as the bricks of my home
Crumble, shatter, split.

A pillar remains standing.
It grows *hair*.

And it speaks, like you and me.
Then, my priestess habits kick in,
And I begin the ritual of slaughter on this speaking, *hairy* pillar.
I pour on a few drops of water,
Like I always do.
And . . . I cry. Like, ugly cry.

    Beat.

I realize . . .
My god,
The pillar is my brother, Orestes!

Why the fuck was he a pillar?
A speaking hairy pillar?!

I mean, Daddy Aggy would always say,
"BOYS ARE THE PILLARS OF A HOUSE."
So . . .
And Orestes is, like, tall, so maybe that's why?
I dunno.

Anyway,
Orestes is dead.

We used to be far apart.
My brother and I.
This was all I could do for him:
Offer droplets in dreams.

CHORUS
(from off stage) PRIESTESS.
IT'S TIME!
WHERE YOU AT?!

IPHIGENIA
Ah. My lady calls.
Yes, I still have ladies.
Was a princess, always a princess.
To work. To work. To work, I go.
Into the temple: where I live,
And where I kill.

> IPHIGENIA *exits, once again*
> *Passing the paper temple.*

SCENE 2.

> ORESTES *and* PYLADES *enter,*
> *Huddled / cuddled,*
> *And hushed.*

> *They are best friends and lovers,*
> *Each others' favourite person in the world.*

ORESTES
Do you see anyone?

PYLADES
(*looks around*) No.

ORESTES
You sure?
Look carefully.

PYLADES
Don't worry.
There's no one here but us . . .
And that . . .

(indicating the temple) What is that?

ORESTES
Ohmygosh
Pylades,
This—
This is the TEMPLE.

PYLADES
This is it?

ORESTES
The goddess's temple,
The one we've journeyed across Argos to find!

PYLADES
We did it, O!

    Beat.

That's wonderful, but . . .
Can we sit a sec, my legs, they're—

ORESTES
Wait.
Don't.
Not safe.
Who knows what these
Taurians are like.

PYLADES
. . . Ugh fine
I'll take a look around.

                                      PYLADES does.

ORESTES
O Phoebus or Apollo,
Whichever you wanna be called today,
You tricky bastard of a god.

What is this land you've brought me to?
You urged me to kill my mother,
To avenge my father.
YOU TOLD ME IT'D BE FINE.

Yet, the furies—
Their furious pursuit filled me with fear,
Quaked my core,
To the point where I prayed to you,
Asked for mercy,
Looked to the sky,
And received your answer of hope:

                    This is spoken by ORESTES, *as if possessed.*

TRAVEL TO TAURIAN LAND.
MY SISTER, ARTEMIS
HAS A REALLY BEAUTIFUL TEMPLE THERE,
(I'VE NOT BEEN)
(I'M BUSY WITH GOD THINGS!)
SHE'S GOT A STATUE THERE,
IT'S MINE!
I ACCIDENTALLY DROPPED IT
WHILE I WAS FLYING THROUGH THE SKY
LIKE
A CENTURY AGO.
I WANT IT BACK!
NOW!
TAKE IT BACK.
BE CLEVER,

OR
BE STRONG.
BRING THE STATUE TO
. . . ATHEEEENNNNNNNNS.
THEN
YOU'LL BE FREE FROM THE FURIES, furies, furies, furies, furies, furies,
Furies, furies.

The voice leaves.

Now I'm here.
Freedom just a statue theft away.
Even the air smells free here.

Beat.

Pylades,
What are we gonna do?

PYLADES
Dude,
I have heard that story, like,
Twenty times now,
The whole ride here . . .
You all right . . . ?

ORESTES
Sorry, it's such an exciting story.

PYLADES
It. really. is.

ORESTES
Oh come on,
You know you love me.

PYLADES
Mmhm.

ORESTES
So what we gonna do,
Partner in crime?

    Beat.

You see those high walls?
Do we have a ladd— /
Do you have a ladder?

PYLADES
No,
Stupid idea.
They'd see us climbing.

ORESTES
Right . . .
Hmm.
Oh!
Do we have a crowbar, we could
Break down the door?

PYLADES
Oh so sorry
Totally forgot to pack
A FRIGGING CROWBAR.

ORESTES
. . . So . . . no?

PYLADES
NO!

Beat.

ORESTES
Uh.
We could make a run for it,
Grab the statue,
And sprint back to the ship?

PYLADES
MY LEGS ARE TIRED.

Beat.

See over there? That cave?

PYLADES points off stage.

I took a look.
No one there.
We can hide,
Keep eyes on the ship.
The distance will keep us safe.

Then,
As soon as it gets dark,
We sneak into the temple,
Grab the statue—

ORESTES
How?

PYLADES
. . . We'll figure it out.

ORESTES
In the dark cave?

PYLADES
In the dark cave.

ORESTES
You're so fucking smart—

PYLADES
Am I? Feels like common sense—

ORESTES
Let's go hide in the dark cave,
You and me.

PYLADES
And?

ORESTES
Rest?
Figure out a plan?

PYLADES
. . . And?

ORESTES
I'll give your legs a rub.
For being so smart.

PYLADES
Why thank you.

> *Beat.*

Just my legs?

ORESTES
If we figure out how to steal the statue, maybe—

PYLADES
Got another *statue* for you—

ORESTES
Oh my god,
You're too much.

> *The boys jet to the dark cave,*
> *Giggling and ripping clothes off of each other.*

SCENE 3.

> *CHORUS enters,*
> *Almost manic in energy,*
> *Funnelled through a stillness,*
> *Like a statue, alive.*

CHORUS
(to audience) Oh, hi.
You're here for the sacrifice—
I mean,
For Iphigenia, right?

> *Beat.*

I say that because
Since our . . .
High Priestess Iffy decided to grace us
With her princess ways,
Our sacrifices have turned into
Quite the spectacle.

Before . . .
We would shepherd all

Them sacrifices,
Throw them up on the altar,
Sever their heads,
And continue on our merry way . . .

Now . . .
Priestess Iffy
Saunters about, taking her time,
Showing off her flowing robes,
Stepping ever so sacredly,
A.k.a., SLOWLY,
Towards our altar,
And taking her sweet-ass time
Tallying the sacrifices' woes and wishes,
Making a show
Of our sacred ritual.
The sacrifices have gotten so long
We have intermissions for peeps to piss.

But hey,
Record numbers.
In droves.
Coming from every which way
To witness
Our Iffy in action.

And that's . . .
A part of me looks at . . .
Looks up to her cuz
She's . . .
Radiant.
And kind.
And thoughtful.

    Beat.

Isn't it the worst when kind people shine?
Ugh.

    Beat.

BUT
SHE'S ALWAYS LATE!
I mean,
I'm always early,
But today's special!

               CHORUS walks around the theatre, or
                         Into the audience, or
                     Takes a step backstage.

Where is Iffy?!

                     CHORUS returns, speaking to us.

Ugh.

I'm not usually alone.
The other ladies caught a cold though,
Flu season, ya know . . .
Woke up this morning
And they were all just:

                     She signals vomiting.

All over the floor.

Poor things under strict stay-at-home orders.
And, like, I feel for them.
Cuz no one wants home to feel like prison.
But on the other hand,

I get to do the cleansing,
The beheading,
The pouring of blood on our
GAWGEOUS statue,
AND the cleanup today!

Yay!

Not only that,
But today
We have two boys from Greece to sacrifice!
Not just any two boys:
A PAIR OF
Hefty, HOT, GREEK homos.
Our Artemis will surely be satisfied.

    Beat.

WHERE IS IPHIGENIA?!

Anyway,
I've been . . . here on Taurian land,
For about . . .
Like at least a millennia,
Maybe two, or a hundred . . .
Who's counting?

I've been at this job since I was a wee babe,
A life devoted to death.

I was primed to be the next High Priestess,
But heeeeeEEEEeeeyyyyy
Iphigenia fell on our lands,
This stunning specimen of royalty,
And the gods passed me over
And gave HER the promotion.

I mean,
I got as much blood rolling around me
As Iphigenia,
Got as much spunk and talent for sacrificial rituals
As her,
Got as much of a story . . .

But.
I got no name.
None.
Mom or Dad, or whatever the fuck made me,
Decided that life would be easier with no name.
They nearly went with Karen,
But they thought better of it.
God bless.

    Beat.

Never thought my lack of a name
Would cost me a promotion . . .
Hey, there's a glass ceiling for us all, ain't there?

    Beat.

You can call me *Chorus.*

Since Iphigenia's . . . "ascension"
I wake up,
Grab coffee,
Go to work,
Chop off heads,
Grab coffee,
Order shawarma,
Go home.
Netflix and chill,
Sleep.

Then it repeats all over and
Over and over and over again.

> *Beat.*

> IPHIGENIA *walks in. Slowly.*

Ah.
FINALLY.
Priestess Iphigenia.
'Sup?

IPHIGENIA
Where are the rest of the ladies?

CHORUS
(gestures and makes sounds of vomiting) Flu season.

IPHIGENIA
Oh shit.
I needed the whole crew today . . .

CHORUS
Why? What's up?

IPHIGENIA
. . .
I can't stop crying.
I can't stop grieving
The ruin of my brother.

CHORUS
What happened?

IPHIGENIA
I saw my brother, Orestes,
In a dream.

CHORUS
Oh, how's he doing?

IPHIGENIA
He's . . . he's dead.

CHORUS
Like his body was like crushed or something?

IPHIGENIA
He wasn't . . . a body in my dream.

CHORUS
What? A cow? A pig?

IPHIGENIA
A . . . pillar.

CHORUS
A pillar?

IPHIGENIA
Yea.

CHORUS
How'd you know it was your brother?

IPHIGENIA
Well, it spoke.

CHORUS
The pillar spoke?

IPHIGENIA
And it had hair.

CHORUS
You spoke to a dead, hairy, communicative pillar,
And you think it was your brother?

IPHIGENIA
Don't mock me.

CHORUS
Hear yourself, *Priestess*.

IPHIGENIA
My brother
Was dead.
So was our house,
And so was my family.
It's all . . . been devastated.

The gods have stolen the only thoughts of hope left
by sending my brother to his grave.

CHORUS
Um. Sorry to hear,
But . . . we do have a job to get / to—

IPHIGENIA
Help me pour these libations.
Here, take this bowl.

CHORUS
We have sacrifices to get to /
Two, in fact.

IPHIGENIA
(interrupting) I'VE GATHERED
Two percent organic milk,
Milked it myself,
The best Taurian wine,
Cinnabon—those were his fav,
Honey of the yellowest bees.

> *Beat.*

These are comforts for the dead.
My brother can enjoy them in the sky.

> *Beat.*

Please, hold it while I pray to my brother:

> CHORUS *reluctantly helps.*

O Orestes,
Take these treats.
I thought these might be more useful, and tasty,
In the afterlife than the usual strands of hair
That people leave for the dead.

O Orestes,
I am so far away from home.
And the people there think I'm dead.
Artemis did a real good job of making the pig

That Daddy Aggy sacrificed look like a real human.
Wonderful cosmetic work, really.

O Orestes,
Rest in peace.
I am so sorry.

> CHORUS *and* IPHIGENIA
> *Pour the libations into the earth.*

CHORUS
Done?

IPHIGENIA
No. We have to sing for him.

CHORUS
Sing?
You're asking me to sing for
The cursed house of Atreus?

IPHIGENIA
Whoa, 'scuse me,
This is my story.
You sing when I tell you to / sing.

CHORUS
Yes . . . Priestess.

IPHIGENIA
But you're right.
Ever since I was born,
I've never tasted luck.
Even coming outta my mother's womb,
Who begat me out of a familial shame— /

CHORUS
(cough cough) / incest /

IPHIGENIA
/ I mean,
Let's not go there,
But even then,
Unlucky at conception.

And now,
Here,
With no partners,
Friends,
Children,
Family,
HOME.

I'm stuck here with you,

CHORUS
Is that so bad?

IPHIGENIA
No, but . . .
Now I'm stuck
Trading in blood,
Offering foreign heads
To foreign gods.
Witnessing cries for help, for mercy,
To please spare me, spare me.
Yet, I feel nothing for them.

CHORUS
Don't feel bad.
It's . . .

One heart in exchange for collective peace.
It's their honour.

IPHIGENIA
They have no choice.

CHORUS
Choice is overrated.

IPHIGENIA
If you had choice
You'd be dead.
Sacrificed at Aulis.

Now
You have your life.
Sacrificing others.
Duty.
Destiny led you to duty.
Cherish it.

    Beat.

Don't . . . don't cry.

    Beat.

IPHIGENIA
I . . .
Thank you . . .

CHORUS
However cursed your family,
Your love for Orestes shines clear as day.

    Beat.

May he rest in peace.
For your sake.

> CHORUS *rests a hand on* IPHIGENIA,
> *A gesture of compassion.*

> *They hum in honour of* ORESTES *and their*
> *Lost families.*

SCENE 4.

> *The tune finishes,*
> *And the libations are done.*
> CHORUS *gets the business moving.*

CHORUS
. . . So we're . . . done?

IPHIGENIA
Mmhm.

CHORUS
You'll be so pleased.
I'm sure it'll cheer you up.
It's a special, special sacrificial day!

IPHIGENIA
Why?

CHORUS
We have TWO boys to offer up
To Artemis today!

IPHIGENIA
What?
Why didn't you tell me earlier!?

CHORUS
You were . . .
Going on
About your hairy pillar of a brother.

IPHIGENIA
Who are these dudes?

CHORUS
I think they're . . . Greek.

IPHIGENIA
How can you tell?

CHORUS
They were . . . Greek-ish.

IPHIGENIA
K.
Any names?

CHORUS
Yes, one of 'em groaned the other's name,
Like
(sexually) Oooooh
PILATES.

IPHIGENIA
Pylades?

CHORUS
Yes. Pilates.

IPHIGENIA
That's a Greek name.

CHORUS
Told you.

IPHIGENIA
What about the other one?

CHORUS
They were climaxing
When I caught them,
Couldn't hear anything but open vowels.

IPHIGENIA
Where did you find them?

CHORUS
They were hiding in the dark cave by the sea.

IPHIGENIA
How did you come upon them?
Tell me.

Flashback.

CHORUS *turns*
And we are by the water.
CHORUS *walks at the edge,*
Closing in towards the dark cave.

The boys are going at it.

ORESTES
(off stage) Oooooh, Pylades!

PYLADES
(off stage) Arrrrrhhhhhhg—

CHORUS
(hears the moans) WTF?

CHORUS *peeks into the dark cave.*

Oh my my.
There's some heat in that hole.

PYLADES
(off stage) Ooooooh no.
Come on, not now!

ORESTES *charges out of the cave.*
He does not see CHORUS.
He is manic, howling, and possessed,
Fighting off imagined Furies.

ORESTES
OOOOH, YOU HELLISH FIGURE,
LEAVE US BE.

DO YOU SEE THAT, PYLADES?
IT WANTS TO KILL ME,
IT WANTS MY HEART.

PYLADES *chases after* ORESTES.

PYLADES
It's nothing, it's nothing,
They're just in your head.
I'm here, you're safe,
Hush hush, I'm right here.

ORESTES
LOOK AT IT'S MOUTH:
LIPS OF FIRE,
TONGUE OF SNAKES,
MY MOTHER'S FACE FOR TEETH.
HELP ME, PYLADES.

ORESTES *falls.*
PYLADES *comforts him.*

PYLADES
There's nothing there,
My sweet,
Nothing . . .

CHORUS *shifts*
And is seen by the boys.

Who's there?!

ORESTES
I TOLD YOU,
HELL ITSELF.

ORESTES
Rushes CHORUS.

DIE. DIE. DIE.

CHORUS
WTF?!

PYLADES
Stop!

ORESTES
RGGGGGG—

CHORUS
STOP!

> *Just at that final*
> *Inch of danger,*
> ORESTES *collapses at* CHORUS*'s feet.*
> PYLADES *stands between them.*
> CHORUS *sighs in relief.*

PYLADES
Wake up!

CHORUS
Um . . .

PYLADES
I'm so so sorry,
Um,
Stranger.
My, um,
Friend,
He . . . well—

> ORESTES *wakes,*
> *Looks up at* CHORUS,
> *And instantly crawls backwards in utter fear.*

ORESTES
. . . Pylades?
WHAT THE FUCK?
What happened?

PYLADES
We were going at it,
You saw the Furies,
Then you attacked this poor stranger!

ORESTES
Oh. I see.
. . . So much for hiding.

> *The boys giggle and*
> *Continue to crawl over each other,*
> *Ready for more.*

> CHORUS *clears her throat.*

> *They stop for a sec.*

Oh. Right.
Sorry, stranger.

CHORUS
All good.

> *Beat.*

You two look a little . . .
Wrecked.

PYLADES
We are.

CHORUS
Just your luck,
Being found on Taurian land.

ORESTES
What do you mean?

CHORUS
We Taurians
Are famously known for our . . .
Hospitality.

PYLADES
Oh wow.

CHORUS
Come with me.
I'll take you to the temple.
We'll take care of you
From . . . head to toe.

PYLADES
Um—

ORESTES
The temple?!
You'll take us inside?!

CHORUS
. . . Sort of.
Well. Yes.

ORESTES
Amazing.

PYLADES
Thank you for the kindness, um . . .

CHORUS
Oh.
I don't have a name,
You can call me Chorus.

ORESTES *and* PYLADES
Are in disbelief over their luck.

ORESTES & PYLADES
Thanks, Chorus!

ORESTES
(approaching CHORUS*)* Can . . . I . . .
May I hug you?

CHORUS *nods.*
An awkward, hilarious hug.

CHORUS
Oh.
Maybe you should put some clothes on.

ORESTES & PYLADES
. . . Give us a sec.

CHORUS
Come with me,
Boiz.

ORESTES, PYLADES, *and* CHORUS *walk towards the temple.*
CHORUS *turns*
And we are back in the present with
IPHIGENIA *and* CHORUS.

Iphigenia,
Offer up these Greeks to Artemis
As vengeance for the slaughter
They planned for you!

    Beat.

IPHIGENIA
Go retrieve the foreigners.
I'll prepare.

CHORUS
Yes,
M'priestess.

                     CHORUS leaves.
             IPHIGENIA is alone on stage.

IPHIGENIA
Oh my lil heart.
"Go retrieve the foreigners,"
Spoken with such casual disregard.
Used to mean something once,
Foreigners,
Used to make my heart ring with kindness
And compassion.
Strange strangers often proved the best conversations.
I would fumble through different languages,
Craving their stories,
Asking for a piece of wisdom unfamiliar in my universe.
Yet now,
"Go retrieve the foreigners,"
A command, an order,
A death sentence.

Truth is, my bad luck and self-pity
Does not lend itself well
To pitying others.

And my fellow is right.
My family wanted me dead.
It was the foreigners, these Taurians,
That took me in,
And let me live in service to their temple.

Here now is the chance
For an eye for an eye:
My sacrifice survived,
Their sacrifice ensured.

To the earth.

Orestes,
See the irony of it all.
Gods who crave the unpolluted
Seek our polluted blood as gifts.
But do we sacrifice ourselves because the gods ask?
Or do we sacrifice our lives because we, humans,
Are blood-hungry rodents, and, excusing ourselves, say:
The gods asked for it, the gods asked for it.

Are the gods evil,
Or are we?

CHORUS returns with the boys.

PYLADES
(starting off stage) You lied to us!

IPHIGENIA
Ooooh, this one's feisty.

ORESTES
Wha-what are you going to—

CHORUS
Spare your words or I'll get the guards.
And trust me,
They'll mess you up.

    Beat.

Ahem.
It is YOUR honour to be offered up
To Artemis,
A once-in-a-lifetime opportunity to—

IPHIGENIA
(under her breath) . . . Literally . . .

CHORUS
Huh?

IPHIGENIA
I said
"Literally,"
It's a once-in-a-lifetime opportunity . . .

    Beat.

Get it?

                              Crickets . . .

. . . Carry on.

CHORUS
It is YOUR honour to be offered up—

ORESTES
Offered / up?

PYLADES
Like, what? Pray?
Become monks?

CHORUS
To be sacrificed.

    Pause.

PYLADES
Holy shit.

    Beat.

ORESTES
Damn.
I'm so sorry, P.

    Beat.

IPHIGENIA
(to CHORUS) You're scaring them.
I'll soothe their souls,
You go and prepare the tools.
I'll join you in a sec.

CHORUS
Yes, m'priestess.

                                         CHORUS goes.

SCENE 5.

IPHIGENIA
So . . . you two are . . .
Friends?

PYLADES
Kinda.

IPHIGENIA
I see.
Well, I send my pity.
I hope you're leaving no one in your family
Brotherless.

ORESTES
Nope.

IPHIGENIA
Where did you two come from?
Must have sailed a long way.

ORESTES
Why do you care?

IPHIGENIA
Curiosity.

PYLADES
Won't you kill us?

IPHIGENIA
Yes.
Still curious.

ORESTES
Doesn't make sense.
You'll kill us,
Yet you pity us.
Make up your mind.

IPHIGENIA
It's made up.
Well, more like
It's decided for me.

    Beat.

Which one of you is Pylades?

PYLADES
(whimpering) Me—

IPHIGENIA
Greek name.
Where from?

ORESTES
Don't answer her, P.

IPHIGENIA
Fine.
Are you two related?

ORESTES & PYLADES
NO.

ORESTES
We're like brothers from a different mother.

PYLADES
Not related at all. Nope.

IPHIGENIA
(to ORESTES) And what is your name, stranger?

ORESTES
. . . Cursed one.

IPHIGENIA
Stop being cheeky.

ORESTES
You're gonna take my body and blood,
I'll keep my name to myself, thank you very much.

IPHIGENIA
God you're so uptight,
So entitled.
Must be rich.

PYLADES
He is.

ORESTES
What the fuck, dude.

IPHIGENIA
Oh, so you think your name is important then?

ORESTES
No.
I wish to die nameless.

IPHIGENIA
Where are you from?

ORESTES
. . .
Earth.

IPHIGENIA
Country? City? Town?
Answer me!

ORESTES
Argos.
We're from Argos.

IPHIGENIA
(stricken by this) Really? You were born there?

ORESTES
In Mycenae, used to be quite nice.

IPHIGENIA
Oh!
You are most welcome here!

PYLADES
. . . Doesn't look it.

IPHIGENIA
Were you exiled, did you two run, or like
Go on a trip and get lost?

ORESTES
Uhhh, we're kinda exiles.

CHORUS walks in.

CHORUS
Priestess,
The tools are ready.

IPHIGENIA
Coming. Coming.
Just have a few more . . .
Uh . . .
Divinations to get through.

CHORUS
Hurry up!
I'm hungry: I want lunch.

CHORUS leaves.

IPHIGENIA
Could I ask you something?

ORESTES
We are your prisoners.

IPHIGENIA
True.
So. Troy.
What happened with Troy?
Did the city get wiped out?

ORESTES
Yes . . .

IPHIGENIA
And . . . Helen . . .
Is she reunited with Menelaus?

ORESTES
Yes.
Their reunion
United me to this fate, now.

IPHIGENIA
Where is she?
She brought me to my fate, here,
Too.

ORESTES
In Sparta.

IPHIGENIA
Ah well,
Good for her . . .

ORESTES
You know so much . . .

IPHIGENIA
Came from Greece . . .
Left when I was a child . . .

    Beat.

What happened to King Agamemnon—

PYLADES
Um.
Don't go there—

ORESTES
He . . .

PYLADES
Shhhhhh

IPHIGENIA
Let him answer!

PYLADES
He's dead. Along with another.

IPHIGENIA
. . . Dead? /
Oh my god.

PYLADES
Why do you care?

IPHIGENIA
He used to have it all.
Such a lucky man.

PYLADES
He was murdered by his wife.
Very lucky indeed.

IPHIGENIA
What?!
How?!

ORESTES
No more questions, please,
Hurts my soul.

IPHIGENIA
Just one more.
Is . . . the wife alive?

ORESTES
She . . . well . . .

PYLADES
Her own son murdered her.

IPHIGENIA
Why?!

PYLADES
To avenge his father,
The son had to kill his mother.

IPHIGENIA
That's . . . that's some fucked-up
Sense of justice.

ORESTES
That justice has followed with a torrent of injustice.

IPHIGENIA
Was Agamemnon survived by any children?

PYLADES
His daughter, Electra.

IPHIGENIA
What about the . . .
The other daughter?

PYLADES
Other . . . daughter?

ORESTES
She's dead.

IPHIGENIA
. . . I see.
Pity that dead sister then . . .

PYLADES
Her death gave life
To Helen.

IPHIGENIA
And Agamemnon's son, the murderer,
Does he live in Argos still?

ORESTES
No.

IPHIGENIA
Where is he?

ORESTES
Running errands for gods.

IPHIGENIA
So he's alive then?!

PYLADES
Yes.

CHORUS re-enters.

CHORUS
The tools are ready.
We await your presence, Priestess.

IPHIGENIA
I'm taking down their families' names,
Just a touch longer.

CHORUS
. . . Sure.

Beat.

I'm gonna grab a bubble tea,
While I wait.

IPHIGENIA
Taro—50% sweet, less ice, please.

> CHORUS *leaves through the audience doors,*
> *Grabs a bubble tea at whatever concession is close by,*
> *Or just like prepared by the stage team outside the theatre.*

Listen.
I have a plan,
Benefits us all.

PYLADES
Set us free?

IPHIGENIA
Sort of.

ORESTES
What do you want?

IPHIGENIA
If I . . .
If I wrote a message,
A letter,
To my family in Argos.
Would you take it to them for me?
I have no one to send the letter with,

And you know the city, we
Clearly have mutual connections.

Freedom in return for a little postal service.

PYLADES
Well what about the sacrifice?
Won't they notice?

IPHIGENIA
Well, not the both of you.
I'll sacrifice you, Pylades,
The law demands it.

PYLADES
What? Ain't fair!

ORESTES
I refuse.
Pylades is my . . .
He's my . . .

>   *Beat.*

Give him the letter.
He can take it to Argos.
He knows the same people I know.
Sacrifice me instead.

There would be no reason to breathe
If not for him.

IPHIGENIA
Oh, wow, dudes, you are seriously in / love.

PYLADES
No. Please.
Spare him.
Take me.

ORESTES
Pylades, please.
I'm the reason we're here.
I'm the reason we got caught.
Live free.

PYLADES
. . .

ORESTES
Priestess.
Take me.

> *IPHIGENIA takes a moment to decide.*
> *There is a weight and gravity to this decision.*

IPHIGENIA
Fine.
Pylades,
You will deliver my letter,
And you,
Cheeky one,
You . . .
You should make peace with your end.

ORESTES
Who will do the deed?

IPHIGENIA
Me, by Artemis's appointment.

ORESTES
Tough gig.

IPHIGENIA
Very.
But good dental.

ORESTES
What will you do?
Chop my head off?

IPHIGENIA
No.
I'mma sprinkle water on you.

ORESTES
Like . . . shower me?

IPHIGENIA.
I said sprinkle, not shower.

ORESTES
Water?

IPHIGENIA
Sacred water. Very sacred.
We have it shipped from the Swiss Alps.

ORESTES
Who will kill me?

IPHIGENIA
The one who's getting bubble tea.

ORESTES
Will I get a grave?

IPHIGENIA
Cremation,
Then ashes scattered as fertilizer.

ORESTES
Oh I wish my sister was here to comfort me . . .

IPHIGENIA
I'll do my best to make it easy for you.
I'll spread more oil than normal,
So that you crisp faster
And reach the sky swiftly.

CHORUS returns.

CHORUS
Sorry.
Lineup.
Ready?

IPHIGENIA
Yes.
I'll follow.

CHORUS exits through the temple.
IPHIGENIA drinks her bubble tea and
Mutters "mmm, so good"
While watching CHORUS leave.

(hushed) Stay here,
Don't try to run,
Or the guards will catch you.
I'll be right back with the letter,
Then you run.
Get to your ship
And deliver my news to Argos.

PYLADES
I . . . sure . . . yea.

> IPHIGENIA *exits through the temple.*
> PYLADES *stares at* ORESTES.
> *Words cannot capture*
> *Their feeling for each other,*
> *And for this goodbye.*

ORESTES
Well?

> *Beat.*

Don't look at me like that.
I don't need pity.
Go home,
Live blessed,
Never forget me.

PYLADES
There is no blessed life without you.

ORESTES
Try.

PYLADES
Can't.
Don't want to.
Let me die with you.

ORESTES
The priestess already showed kindness,
To ask more would be futile.

PYLADES
She knew so much . . .

ORESTES
Yes.
Such pity she showed Father,
As if she knew Daddy Aggy herself . . .
Why did she care so much about Argos?

PYLADES
Must be from there.

ORESTES
Or read the news.

PYLADES
True,
Hard to forget what you did to your mother.

ORESTES
Asshole.

PYLADES
I'm *your* asshole.

ORESTES
Go home and spread your ass cheeks far and wide.

PYLADES
If I go home,
They'll make me move in with Electra.
I don't wanna live with your sister.
I wanna marry you.
I wanna breathe my last breaths with you.
I wanna burn on the pyre with you.
Let us end, together.

ORESTES
This is my doing,
Don't take this on.
When you go home,
Make babies with Electra,
Then I'll live on through your children.

PYLADES
That's fucked.

ORESTES
No. Go. Live!
Keep my father's house.
I'll be cremated here,
But gimme a burial there.
Have Electra pour libations for me,
Tell her some Greek woman sacrificed me.

    Beat.

Bye, P.
You are the dearest thing
To grace my life.
Thank you for—

PYLADES
I promise, yes, I promise
To never betray Electra;
I promise to keep your pa's* home;
I promise to bury you.
You are the luck of my life.

---

* Should be substituted for whatever word stands for "father" in the performer's ancestral tongue.

They embrace.
Kiss.
Hold each other as if it's the last.

SCENE 6.

IPHIGENIA walks in.
She strips paper from the temple walls.
Folds it.
It becomes the letter.

IPHIGENIA
Don't stop because of me.
You can hold each other.
I don't mind.

PYLADES & ORESTES
(staggered) Thank you, Priestess.

IPHIGENIA
You're welcome.

   Beat.

Here's the letter,
Take it.
But swear an oath, in front of me here,
That you will do as promised.

ORESTES
Will you swear an oath in return?

IPHIGENIA
About what?

ORESTES
Promise safe passage for Pylades.

IPHIGENIA
How else is he gonna deliver the letter?
Duh.

ORESTES
What do you think, P?

PYLADES
. . . What do you want me to say, Priestess?

IPHIGENIA
"I will deliver this letter to your family."

PYLADES
"I will deliver this letter to your family."

IPHIGENIA
And I will deliver you home.

PYLADES
. . . Wait.
What happens if,
Like,
There's a storm,
And the ship is flinging every which way,
And the letter gets swept up by the wind and the waves?
If I had only the choice to save myself or the letter,
What do I do then?
The oath would be broken.

IPHIGENIA
Here.
I'll read you the letter.
Do you have a good memory?

PYLADES
Sorta.

ORESTES
He does.

PYLADES
I do?

ORESTES
Without you, I'd be perpetually lost.

IPHIGENIA
Well, remember these words,
Repeat them to my loved ones
If somehow the letter and you get
Battered by waves.

PYLADES
I'll do my best.
Who's the letter for?

IPHIGENIA
Orestes.

    Beat.

Give this letter to Electra,
Tell her to hold onto it until
His return.

The boys freeze.

What?

PYLADES
Nothing.

ORESTES
Continue.

IPHIGENIA
Orestes, son of Agamemnon:
"Hey, Orestes,
Iphigenia sends word.
The sister you thought was slaughtered at Aulis,
She's alive.
Long story,
Mistaken pigs, flying gods,
Was a princess,
Now a priestess."

ORESTES
Where is she? What?
How is she alive?

IPHIGENIA
She's right here.

ORESTES
Huh?

IPHIGENIA
It's me, you dumb fuck.
Now stop interrupting.
Pylades, listen close:
"Brother, bring me back to Argos before I die, I beg you.

I am stuck here in Taurian land and
I am trapped as Priestess,
Slaughtering strangers by law!
Free me,
Or I'll set a curse on you,
Orestes."

Remember that name, P, that's why I said it thrice.

PYLADES
Noted. Thanks.

ORESTES
Oh my god.

IPHIGENIA
Oh my god what?
Stop interrupting,
Poor P won't be able to remember
Any of this.

ORESTES
Nothing.
Sorry.

IPHIGENIA
Uh. K.
(back to PYLADES) "I'm alive,
Brother,
I'm alive.
Love, your sister, always.
Iphigenia."

PYLADES
You're a good writer.

IPHIGENIA
Didn't have much time.

PYLADES
It's beautiful, just beautiful.

IPHIGENIA
Did you memorize it?

PYLADES
Oh yes.
I'll never forget this.

IPHIGENIA
Huh?

> PYLADES *takes the letter from* IPHIGENIA,
> *Turns,*
> *Hands it to* ORESTES.

PYLADES
A letter for you.
Could be junk mail, I dunno.

IPHIGENIA
What?

ORESTES
. . .

IPHIGENIA
What's happening?

PYLADES
. . . Say something!
You're just staring at her!

ORESTES
I . . .

IPHIGENIA
What happened to him?
Is this like what happened back on the beach?

ORESTES
Sister.

IPHIGENIA
. . .
Orestes?
. . .

> ORESTES *runs to hold* IPHIGENIA.

IPHIGENIA
Don't get your snot and tears on my robes,
It's very delicate cloth.

ORESTES
Sister!

IPHIGENIA
You can't be . . .
I saw . . .
You were . . .
Who's your mother?

ORESTES
Clytemnestra.
Daughter of Tyndareus.

IPHIGENIA
What's her nickname?

ORESTES
Clem.

IPHIGENIA
Everyone knew her nickname.

ORESTES
She called you Iffy,
Electra called you Icky,
I called you PRINCESS.

IPHIGENIA
How . . . do you . . .

ORESTES
Remember your bath at Aulis,
Before your . . . well,
Supposed sacrifice?

IPHIGENIA
The water was so fucking hot,
I thought I'd be boiled alive.
Dead before the sacrifice.

ORESTES
Yes,
And you leaned over to Clem,
And said,
"I hope the heavens treat me better."

IPHIGENIA
And then your little hand . . .
You were what,
Like, eleven?
God you had such small hands,
Even for an eleven-year-old.

ORESTES
I was TEN.

IPHIGENIA
Still, they were . . .
Particularly tiny.

ORESTES
Well,
It fit right into your palm,
So . . . whatever.

IPHIGENIA
Yes,
It was perfect.
Your little hand in mine,
As you walked with me up the altar.

ORESTES
I didn't wanna let go of you.

IPHIGENIA
Daddy Aggy had to rip you away.
Gosh you were such a crybaby.
It was honestly kinda embarrassing.

ORESTES
I couldn't watch.

IPHIGENIA
And you couldn't stop it.

ORESTES
I . . . I never never never
Let go of the guilt . . .
I'm so so so so sorry, sister.

IPHIGENIA
You were ten.
I blame Clem and Aggy,
Not you.
And . . .
Well.
Now you can live guilt-free!

ORESTES
Well . . .
Not sure about that . . .
"Living" and "guilt-free" part just yet . . .

　　Pause.

　　　　　　　　　　　　　　　　IPHIGENIA and ORESTES
　　　　　　　　　　　　　　　　Burst out laughing,

IPHIGENIA
My . . . brother.
I never thought I'd . . .
This is . . .
To see you again.
I—

ORESTES
To see *you* again, sister.

　　　　　　　　　　　　They hold each other in silence.
　　　　　　　　　　　　　　PYLADES *watches, moved.*
　　　　　　　　　　They are crying in each others' arms,
　　　　　　　　　　　　　　　　And then laughing,
　　　　　　　　　　They are laughing / crying out of
　　　　　　　　　　　　　　　　　　Pure joy.

SCENE 7.

They release the embrace.

IPHIGENIA
Happiness, from now on, I pray.

ORESTES
Blessed to be reunited,
Cursed in circumstance,
Yet again.

IPHIGENIA
Yet again, indeed,
Since that day
Daddy Aggy went for my throat,
I knew that curses run thick in the blood.
In *our* blood.

ORESTES
I cannot forgive Father for that.

IPHIGENIA
Yet, you avenged him by killing Mother.

ORESTES
You may never forgive me for that.

IPHIGENIA
Forgiveness is possible, as long as we're alive.

ORESTES
Just a few moments longer, and if not for P here,
You'd have killed your own brother!

IPHIGENIA
That wouldn't be surprising, honestly.

ORESTES
Not at all.

They share a laugh.
CHORUS comes out.
They quickly shuffle apart.

IPHIGENIA
Ahem.
Now say your final words, before . . .
Before I lead you to the altar . . .

PYLADES
Yes, Priestess . . .

ORESTES
Miracles happen, thank you, god.

CHORUS
What's that one going on about?
Furies got him?

IPHIGENIA
The shock of it all,
It's overwhelming,
Defence mechanism,
I dunno.
Weirdo.

CHORUS
The knife is sharpened,
The king awaits.

Finish the prayers
And join us at the altar.

CHORUS goes.

PYLADES
You two are very sweet,
But shut up,
Catch up later,
We have to go.

IPHIGENIA
You shut up.
I've been dreaming of this day forever!

PYLADES
I don't want to die!

ORESTES
Sister,
There must be a way out?
Do you know where our ship is?

IPHIGENIA
Hmmm . . .
The king would have seized it by now.

    Beat.

Wait!
What happened to Electra?

ORESTES
Oh, she got married.

IPHIGENIA
Ooooh to who?

ORESTES
Him.

ORESTES points at PYLADES.

PYLADES
Marriage is just a title.
We don't do anything.
Well, I mean, I left her behind when I—

IPHIGENIA
Well, hello, husband of Electra,
Boyfriend of Orestes.
You are favoured by the house of Atreus.

PYLADES
Lucky me—

IPHIGENIA
So how'd you end up here?

ORESTES
Running from the Furies.

IPHIGENIA
Impossible.

ORESTES
That's how it felt at first,
Endless torment.
But in seeking a way to escape the
Furies we ended up at Phoebus's / lodging—

IPHIGENIA
Phoebus?—

PYLADES
He means Apollo—

ORESTES
And *Phoebus* rose up and / up—

PYLADES
No. Please.
No, not / again.

ORESTES
Up and up,
A god's voice rendering destiny:

> PYLADES *mimics / mocks*
> *The following Phoebus speech behind* ORESTES.

TRAVEL
TO TAURIAN LAND.
I FLEW OVER IT ONCE,
ACCIDENTALLY DROPPED A STATUE THERE.
CAN YOU GET IT FOR ME?
BRING IT TO ATHENS.
THEN YOU'LL BE FREE FROM THE FURIES, furies, furies, etc.

And that was that.
Here we are.

> *Beat.*

Wait.
Do you know where the statue is?

IPHIGENIA
Oh yes.

ORESTES
Then help us.
Help me win my freedom from the Furies.
We can go home together!
We just have to steal the statue,
Bring it to Athens,
Then I'll be Fury-free!

IPHIGENIA
Way ahead of you.
I've dreamed of returning to Argos
Since being here.
I must find a way to hide you from the king,
To access the statue,
And to get us to the beach.

How does one avoid predetermined death?

ORESTES
Kill the king?

IPHIGENIA
Don't make murder a habit, brother.
And to murder a host,
You'd lose one set of Furies and gain another.

PYLADES
Hide us here somewhere?
Escape when it's dark?

IPHIGENIA
The king's guards
will catch us.

They're like obsessed with me,
So they watch my every step.

ORESTES
How then?

IPHIGENIA
I GOT IT.

ORESTES
What?

IPHIGENIA
We can wield our cursed past!
Manipulate your matricide for our use!

ORESTES
WOMEN ARE SO GOOD AT SCHEMING—

IPHIGENIA
. . . Uh . . . okay . . .

> *Beat.*

I'll announce how you murdered Mother—

ORESTES
Wow, I know we just reunited, but like
That's personal.

IPHIGENIA
You're tainted,
Unfit for sacrifice.
Impure.

ORESTES
Thanks so much.

IPHIGENIA
Unholy.

ORESTES
I get it,
You can stop now.

IPHIGENIA
I will propose to wash you both with sea water,
Say how the salt
Cleanses impurities.

ORESTES
What about the statue?

IPHIGENIA
Hmm . . .
I'll have to get my fellow in on this,
Say how . . .
Your presence has warped the statue with
Impurity.
How it's . . . it's been
Touched by the Furies . . .
How it'll need a wash and a scrub.
Then
We'll take it with us,
Head directly to the beach.
There must be a ship we can use . . .
THEN, FREEDOM.

ORESTES
I'll say it again,
Cuz hot damn you're brilliant:
WOMEN ARE SO GOOD AT SCHEMING.

    Beat.

PYLADES
What about me?

IPHIGENIA
What about you?

PYLADES
What excuse will you use to
Cleanse me?

IPHIGENIA
You're gay!

PYLADES
So?

IPHIGENIA
The world sees you as impure.

PYLADES
Not everyone.

IPHIGENIA
No, of course not,
You two are the cutest things I've seen in ages,
But,
This world is unkind to anything that confuses.

PYLADES
I'm not confused.

IPHIGENIA
Nor should you be,
But it is certainly a reason to give the king,
Say your blood is impure to offer the goddess.

They laugh awkwardly.
PYLADES *laughs and laughs.*
And then it turns:

PYLADES
Sure sure,
I'm used to it.
My grandma needed blood.
I offered to donate,
Seeing how we shared the same blood type.
The hospital said no.
Cuz I get fucked up the ass.
So Grandma got blood from a stranger instead.
How odd, to
Think a stranger would be more fitting for
A family's need for blood simply because
I love who I love.

ORESTES
. . . Pylades.

PYLADES
I'm all right.
I almost wish I had a reason like yours,
I KILLED MY MOTHER, something like that.
A reason borne out of circumstance and tragic fate, yes,
But at least not a reason I was born into.

CHORUS begins to slowly
Prowl towards the group.

ORESTES
I was born into this fate.

PYLADES
You know what I mean.

ORESTES
Are you jealous . . . ?

PYLADES
No.
I love you.
I'm not jealous.
But even in our relationship,
You're the main character.
Always.
You're the "MAN," whatever the fuck that means.
You're the TOP—I KNOW exactly what the fuck that means.
And you're the hero.
And I'll—

ORESTES
You're my hero. You're my all—

PYLADES
Listen to me!

Beat.

I'll be P.
I'll be little gay boy sidekick:
An appetizer,

A piece
Of your whole—

ORESTES
You're my hole!

PYLADES
WHOLE. Like WHOLE FOODS.

    Beat.

That too.
I'm your brain.

ORESTES
Come here.

PYLADES.
No.

ORESTES
Sidekick, appetizer, holes, bottom, heroes,
All these descriptors . . .

    Beat.

To me:
You're more than anything the world can define,
You're Pylades.
The Pylades that gets me through thick and thin.
The P in my PB and J / sandwich—

PYLADES
Ohmygod, shutthefuckup—

ORESTES
And you're . . .

    Beat.

I am no hero,
No man,
No nothing
Without you.

I think you're everything.

    Beat.

PYLADES
You're TOO MUCH.

ORESTES
Now come here, lemme kiss your sweet cheeks—

IPHIGENIA
Not now, boys. My fellow, she's back . . .

SCENE 8.

        CHORUS enters.

CHORUS
Hi.

IPHIGENIA, PYLADES, & ORESTES
. . . Hi.

CHORUS
Sup?
Ready for slaughter?
My hands are itching for some—

IPHIGENIA
I . . . I have a favour to ask—

CHORUS
Oh?

IPHIGENIA
These . . . boys,
I've . . . uh . . . interrogated
Their souls,
And man,
They bring with them
Some forbidden sin!
If . . . if we slaughter them,
As is,
I FEAR their blood will
Release upon our Taurian comrades
The plague of man-on-man love—

    PYLADES sighs.

Of transgressions that . . .
That are so fucked-up,
I dare not speak them!

CHORUS
Oh, like what?
Be specific.

IPHIGENIA
Of . . . Of
Familial murder!

CHORUS
Be. Specific.

IPHIGENIA
Well, this man,
He murdered his mother—

ORESTES
To avenge my father!

IPHIGENIA
Oooooooh
How dare you speak,
Greekish fool
Oh see . . . see this as evidence
Of an unrepentant soul!

CHORUS
I don't see a problem with sacrificing them—

IPHIGENIA
I FEAR THEIR BLOOD WILL—

CHORUS
I highly doubt that matricide
Is contagious—

IPHIGENIA
Oh just shut up and listen, / goddammit!

CHORUS
Sorry?

IPHIGENIA
I mean,
My fellow . . .
As they breathed their story to life,
I trembled with unholy thoughts
And felt our statue
Resonating with some dark ring.
I believe we must cleanse our statue
And these boys
With our sacred sea water
Before their sacrifice.

    Beat.

> *A pregnant pause,*
> *Air sucked in, as all await*
> CHORUS*'s response.*

CHORUS
If you say so.

    Beat.

IPHIGENIA
Oh. Well . . .
That was / easy.

CHORUS
You ARE our High Priestess.
I have no reason to doubt your
Holy faculties.

IPHIGENIA
Great.
Then.
Please. Go grab the statue,
Bring it to me.

CHORUS
Why can't you grab it?

IPHIGENIA
I must keep watch over these boys.
I am holding their darkness at bay.

CHORUS
How?

IPHIGENIA raises her hands
And mumbles some very elaborate jargon

IPHIGENIA
Ohhhhhhhh
Artemis protects us!

CHORUS
I see.
Well,
I'll be back with the—

IPHIGENIA
Go!

CHORUS
. . . Yes.
M'priestess.

CHORUS steps off
To retrieve the statue.
The three huddle together,
Dropping their act.

IPHIGENIA
So.
Here's what we'll do.
When she gets back,
I'll go right up to her,
Thank her,
Mumble some prayers on her.
I'll get her to close her eyes,
Then! Pylades, you knock her out,
And, brother, you grab the statue.
We'll sneak through the back
And make a run for it.
Sound good?

PYLADES
Yea yea.

ORESTES
Fuck,
P, We're gonna be free!

ORESTES swings PYLADES by the hips,
Lays a gorgeous kiss down.

ORESTES
Thank you for everything—

PYLADES
I can't wait to go home—

IPHIGENIA
Shhhh, not now!

ORESTES
Oh, sister,
I can't wait for you to see the fam again.
Electra is gonna FREAK—

IPHIGENIA
Uh—

ORESTES
WOMEN ARE SO GODDAMN GOOD AT —

SCENE 9.

CHORUS returns with the statue.

ORESTES
SCHEMING.

PYLADES
(to ORESTES) Shhhh . . .

CHORUS
Heyo.

IPHIGENIA, PYLADES, & ORESTES
(staggered) . . . Hi.

IPHIGENIA
Thank you for grabbing the—

CHORUS
What scheme?

    Beat.

IPHIGENIA
Huh?

CHORUS
That one.
He said,
Well, more like
He screamed,
"Scheming."

ORESTES
I uh . . .

PYLADES
You misheard—

CHORUS
I didn't ask you—

IPHIGENIA
He didn't say—

ORESTES
I meant—

PYLADES
Screaming. He said / screaming—

IPHIGENIA
Yes exactly. Screaming—

CHORUS
No . . . I'm pretty sure
I heard—

ORESTES
SEMEN.

    Beat.

CHORUS
Excuse me?
. . . Semen?

    Beat.

ORESTES
Yes.
I said . . .
. . .
. . . Semen.

CHORUS
Um.
In what . . . context?

ORESTES
Uh.

PYLADES
We are
Seamen. We—

ORESTES
Yes, we / seamen—

PYLADES
Come from the sea.

ORESTES
Yes.
We sail the seas,
And—

PYLADES
Men of the sea.

ORESTES
And we are just so . . .
Embarrassed that we
Crashed our ship on Taurian shores,
As . . . seamen and everything—

PYLADES
Yea. God. So embarrassing.

ORESTES
. . . Anyway.

IPHIGENIA
Ahem.
Yes.
Anyway.
The statue.
Thank you, fellow.

IPHIGENIA *walks up to* CHORUS.
PYLADES *and* ORESTES *follow behind.*

CHORUS
Sure.

IPHIGENIA
Oh, my fellow,
I fear just being in their presence
Is enough to infect the soul.
Here,
Before we head out for the cleansing,
Let us pray the gay away.

    Beat.

Here, this . . . boy,
Let him hold it while I pray for you.

                ORESTES reaches out for the statue.
                              A moment.
             FREEDOM JUST A GRAB AWAY!

ORESTES
Yes . . .
Let me hold it—

CHORUS
Fuck off.

THE PLAY BREAKS

        IPHIGENIA, PYLADES, and ORESTES
                      Stand shocked.

IPHIGENIA
Do as you're told,
Fellow.

CHORUS
Stop lying to me.

IPHIGENIA
Excuse me?
I'm your High Priestess
This is MY story.
Give us the statue.

CHORUS
Why?

IPHIGENIA
I told you we need to cleanse it.

CHORUS
No.
You're lying.
I know your plan.
You wanna steal it and leave Tauros.
Isn't that right?

Oh shit, their plan has been revealed!

IPHIGENIA
Fellow, I finally have a chance to go home
And all I need is / this statue . . .

CHORUS
This is your home!
Will you throw in my face
All the
KINDNESS
That I
Have shown you?

IPHIGENIA
But this is my family.

CHORUS
Such loyalty for the bloodline
That wished for your sacrifice.
A bloodline so thick.
Thick in curses.
Thick with hypocrisies.
Thick with lies.

    Beat.

You're one of us!

We have nurtured you
On this land.
Here you are now,
Plotting to steal
And run with these people.

PYLADES
But you want to kill us!

CHORUS
It is an honour to be sacrificed.
Nothing like your mindless cycle of vengeance.
And our ritual is meant to protect our home;
Would you not do the same?

PYLADES
I don't want to die!

ORESTES
Do not get in our way.

CHORUS
You think this will
Free you from your guilt?
The statue has no ability to do that!

ORESTES
It's a decree from Phoebus.
This statue is meant for his temple in Athens.
It was just . . . misplaced here on Taurian *land*.
This is my mission, fellow, by a god's decree!

CHORUS
Your god.
Not mine.

And this story you tell
About your god dropping the statue here,
That's a lie too.

You tell yourself whatever you need
To justify your injustice.

ORESTES
THIS STATUE IS MY FREEDOM.

CHORUS
This statue
Is a pillar
Of our very culture.

I have watched over this statue for a millennium.
It has survived wars,
Massacres,
Genocides,
Extinctions,

Birth of tyrants,
And the death of nations.

We pray to it for calm seas,
Worship it for bountiful harvest,
Measure our feet in dance when babes are born.

And you want to steal it.

ORESTES
(to IPHIGENIA) We can still make a run for it!
(to PYLADES) DROP HER!

CHORUS
Go for it.

To ORESTES:

If the guilt of killing your mother isn't enough
Of a curse,
Your theft of this statue
Will solidify your living damnation.

To PYLADES:

If you think your love for a mother killer
Shields you from guilt,
Know that your silent complicity in this taints you too.

To IPHIGENIA:

If after all the duty I've shown you,
Priestess,
Your recompense for hospitality
Is violence.

If my articulation of this statue's significance
Is insignificant to you.
Then go for it.
Compound your story of familial murder
With the transgression of
FUCKING COLONIALISM.

IPHIGENIA
I never asked to be here!
I never wanted to be Priestess!
I have
A chance to return home,
A chance to redeem my story,
And I'm going to take it.
Please.

> *Beat.*

CHORUS
Fine.
But some stories must not continue.

All three of you come from families
Written from myths,
Drawn from stones,
From paintings,
Figures that live beyond everybody,
Have been given free pass
To flaunt your history
And repeat your stories.

We can stop this cycle now.
Let it end here.

PYLADES

. . . Orestes . . . this doesn't feel right . . .

(to CHORUS) He's . . . he's just having a bad day, he's not usually like—

CHORUS

When I have a bad day,
I order shawarma.
I mix it up.
I get two, three, sometimes four of 'em.
I wolf 'em down.
I eat the pain away.
I yell into a pillow.
I scratch at my scabs.
I grind my teeth smooth.
I take that
RAGE
And it twists and ferments and bubbles and
It sleeps, roaring in my
Rest.

When I have a bad day,
I don't fucking steal statues
And shit supremacy on strangers.

GROW THE FUCK UP.

PYLADES

Orestes, let's go, please.
Love, please,
I fear what will become of you—

ORESTES

SHUT UP, P. /
You know me.
Don't side with this foreigner!

CHORUS
There it is.
There. it. is.

Easier to rip my throat out
When you think me foreign
And devoid of humanity.

PYLADES
/ Whoa. We never said that! /

IPHIGENIA
Calm down, Orestes,
The Chorus, they've . . .
Kept me safe,
Took care of me,
Treated me like one of their own.

    Beat.

Fellow,
We're the foreigners here.
We don't belong here.
We want to go home.

CHORUS
Ah, Priestess.
So easy to claim what's home and what's not.
When royalty and divine favours
Guide your way.

    Beat.

But family is family,
I get it.

We cannot compare with
Blood bonds.

Beat.

Out of care and friendship,
I'll let you and your brother
Leave.
I'll forgo my duty of sacrifice—just this once.
(to ORESTES) But.
You, go.
Don't play into your myth.
Leave the statue.
Face your Furies.
Let us make space for something new.

PYLADES
Orestes, let's just go, let's just—

IPHIGENIA
Brother, this is our way out, this is
Freedom without ferocity.

ORESTES *thinks and thinks.*

ORESTES
. . . No.
No. no. no. no. no.
I've travelled too far—

PYLADES
We can travel back—

ORESTES
I've harmed too many—

IPHIGENIA
We've been harmed too—

ORESTES
I've pursued all this, all this . . .
For you to just dismiss it,
Reduce all I've seen,
All I've done,
All I've resisted
As mere myth?

   Beat.

Fuck off.
You don't know what it's like to
Wake every night
Haunted by those faceless Fury fucks
Spitting curses down my spine.

I've harmed cuz I've been harmed.
I will harm again.

I will grapple with all of that
However the fuck I want.

That statue will set me free
Today, right now.
Maybe not forever,
But right now.
None of you get to tell me
How to live my story.

GIVE. ME. THE. STATUE.

                                 ORESTES rages,
                 Corners CHORUS *throughout this text.*

> *IPHIGENIA and* ORESTES *can chime in with*
> *"Whoa" / "Calm down" / "*WTF*" / or try to physically*
> *Hold him back.*

GIVE. ME. THE. STATUE.

YOU NAMELESS BASIC.
I REGRET NOT RIPPING YOU APART
BACK AT THE BEACH.
TAKE YOUR MORALS,
TAKE YOUR FOREIGN TAURIAN ASS,
AND ROT.
THERE'S A SPECIAL PLACE FOR YOU IN HELL,
AND I'MMA SEND YOU STRAIGHT DOWN
TO BURN.

GIVE IT TO ME.

> ORESTES *wrestles the statue from*
> CHORUS *and*
> *Injures them in the process,*
> *Leaving them on the ground, hurt.*

CHORUS
No!

> ORESTES *relishes in his accomplished mission.*
> *It's as if he's possessed by a Fury.*
> *How passionate he is in his freedom.*

ORESTES
YES.
FUCK YOU, FURIES.
FUCKKKKK YOUUUUUUUUUUUUU.
I'M DONE WITH YOU.
DONE WITH SHAME.

DONE WITH SLAUGHTER.
DONE WITH REPENTANCE.
DONE WITH ERRANDS FOR GODS.
DONE WITH FEAR.

TRY HAUNTING ME NOW,
YOU FURIES!
I DARE YOU.
STICK THIS UP YOUR ASS.
I'M FREE.
I'M FREE.
I'M FREE.

    Beat.

Pylades,
I'mma make you the happiest man
In this wide wide world.

PYLADES
. . .

IPHIGENIA
. . . You're . . .
You're vicious.

ORESTES
Oh come on,
WE'RE FREE!
Let's book it to the beach.

    ORESTES grabs PYLADES.
    While exiting with PYLADES:

Follow me, Iffy!

Home!

ORESTES and PYLADES exit.

IPHIGENIA slowly follows . . .
But as she passes the CHORUS:

IPHIGENIA
I'm . . . I'm sure you'll find some
Other statue or rock or tree or whatever
To worship?

CHORUS
You know that's not how this works.

ORESTES returns to grab IPHIGENIA.

ORESTES
Iffy! Let's go!

IPHIGENIA goes.

SCENE 10.

CHORUS is left alone on stage.

CHORUS
How disappointing . . .
How typical.
How completely, utterly, wholly
Typical.

The same cycle,
The same crime,
The same heroes,
The same story:

> CHORUS *sustains this for as long*
> *As inhumanly possible*
> *(And within the limits of bearability).*
> *This must increase in tempo until it's racing by the end.*
> *It grows into a giant roar.*

Over and over and over and over and over and over and over and
over and over and over and over and over and over and over and over
and over and over and over and over and over and over and over
and over and over and over and over and over and over and over and
over and over and over and over and over and over and over and over
and over and over and over and over and over and over and over and
over and over and over and over and over and over and over and over
and over and over and over and over and over and over and over and
over and over and over and over and over and over and over and over
and over and over and over and over and over and over and over and
OVER AGAIN.

END.

ANTIGONE: 方

Antigone: 方 was first produced by Young People's Theatre, Toronto, from April 29 to May 16, 2019, with the following cast and creative team:

Antigone/Chorus: Jasmine Chen
Ismene/Chorus: Rachel Mutombo
Guard/Chorus: Christopher Allen
Teo/Chorus: Aldrin Bundoc
Haemon/Chorus: Simon Gagnon
Tiresia/Chorus: Soo Garay
Kreon/Chorus: John Ng
Neikes/Chorus: Jeff Yung

Directors: Stephen Colella and Karen Gilodo
Set and Costume Design: Christine Urquhart
Lighting Design: Rebecca Picherack
Sound Design: David Mesiha
Movement Director: Viv Moore
Stage Manager: Kate Duncan

CHARACTERS

Antigone
Ismene
Haemon
Kreon
Neikes and Teo
Tiresia
Guard
Speakerphone (a pre-recorded voice)

The Chorus is ever-present throughout this version of *Antigone* and doubles with the main cast. The premiere production at Young People's Theatre used the following double casting:

Ismene + Chorus 3
Haemon + Chorus 2
Teo + Chorus 4
Neikes + Chorus 1
Tiresia + Chorus 7
Kreon + Chorus 6
Guard + Chorus 5

The suggested breakdown for sections with Chorus A and Chorus B is as follows:

Chorus A
Chorus 4
Chorus 6
Chorus 5
Chorus 3

Chorus B
Chorus 1
Chorus 2
Chorus 7
Antigone (for the beginning sections, as an extra body in the Chorus)

SETTING

We are in a country not quite like ours, but not quite so different either. A country where censorship is the norm, state broadcasts are made through speakerphones, rain is seen more than sun, televisions play what we need to see, the news is no news at all, and people disappear when their voices squeak a tone too loudly.

PROLOGUE.

A typical morning at the re-education centre:
A morning ritual led by TIRESIA;
A series of call and responses
With the re-educatees kneeling / standing /
In a position of supplication,
With their arms outstretched.
They are smiling against their will.

GUARDS circle the
Re-educatees.

TIRESIA
Glory to the Supreme Leader!

ALL
Glory to the Supreme Leader.

TIRESIA
He has led us through a thousand years of
Sweeping glory!

ALL
He has led us through a thousand years of
Sweeping glory!

TIRESIA
May he will it!

ALL
May he will it . . .

TIRESIA
Glory to the Supreme Leader!

ALL
Glory to the Supreme Leader.

TIRESIA
He has led us through a thousand years of
Sweeping glory!

ALL
He has led us through a thousand years of
Sweeping glory!

TIRESIA
May he will it!

ALL
May he will it . . .

> *This may continue and repeat*
> *In various sequences until*
> *One of the re-educatee's arms sag,*
> *The* GUARD *is quick to move over*
> *And reprimand them.*

GUARD
Arms up!

TIRESIA
May he will it!

ALL
May he will it . . .

> *The re-educatee*
> *Smiles in response,*
> *But is fighting fatigue.*
> *Their arms tremble.*

GUARD
I said, arms up!

> *TIRESIA walks over*
> *And places a hand on the GUARD.*

> *For a moment,*
> *Their attention wanes from the*
> *Re-educatees.*

TIRESIA
Leave her be,
Young man.

GUARD
But, ma'am—

TIRESIA
Her arms are tired,
But her spirit
Soars for our Leader.
That is most important,
Wouldn't you say?

GUARD
. . . Yes, ma'am—

> *Behind the* GUARD *and* TIRESIA*'s back,*
> NEIKES *and* TEO *exchange glances,*
> *A plan set in motion.*

TIRESIA
Let's continue:
May he will it!

ALL
May he will it . . .

TIRESIA
May he will it!

ALL
May he—

> *At this distraction,*
> NEIKES *leaps up,*
> HAEMON *follows,*
> *And they pull the* GUARD *to the ground,*
> *Knocking him out.*

NEIKES
Tiresia,
Don't move!

> NEIKES *holds a stance,*
> *Readied against* TIRESIA.

TIRESIA
Put down your weapon.

> *He doesn't.*

NEIKES
Don't move!

Haemon.
Follow through the back gates,
Grab their weapons,
Release our allies.

 Beat.

We'll reunite at the square.

 Beat.

RUN.
GO.

HAEMON
Come with me—

NEIKES
I have to get my ma.
Go, before the alarms—

SPEAKERPHONE
BREACH.
THE SEVEN GATES OF
THE CENTRE HAVE BEEN
BREACHED.

NEIKES
Haemon, GO!

SPEAKERPHONE
BREACH.

> *HAEMON stumbles towards the exit.*
> *Pause.*

NEIKES
Tiresia,
Release my ma!

TIRESIA
Release her?
She's under my protection.

NEIKES
How?
By locking her up in an isolation chamber?
How is that protection?

TIRESIA
She has her life.
So do you.
You're fed.
You're allowed sport.

That's my promise to all at the centre:

Life.

Better than the alternative,
Wouldn't you say?

SPEAKERPHONE
Breach.

NEIKES
Stop mocking us!
You lead this hell on earth!

TIRESIA
Hell is for the dead.
You're alive.
Be grateful.

> *Beat.*

The Supreme Leader is not as . . . merciful as I am,
As you well know.

SPEAKERPHONE
BREACH.

NEIKES
Release Ma.
Release her.
NOW.

TIRESIA
You will be caught.
Punished.
Executed.

NEIKES
Let me take her with me.

TIRESIA
You will be putting her in danger!
In here, I can guard her life,
Make sure she's fed,
That she has the right medication!

She's . . .
You and I both know she's not capable of leaving!

NEIKES
I would rather that risk
Than to leave her here to rot
With you.

SPEAKERPHONE
BREACH.

TIRESIA
I will take care of her,
I promise.

> *NEIKES spits on TIRESIA.*
> *Pause.*

NEIKES
Coward.

We called you Aunty.
We treated you like family.
Our ma saw you as a sister.

You erased her memories,
And now you're telling me to be grateful that she's alive?!

Once our comrades reach the square,
We will reveal the truth.
We will tell the world
That re-education is a lie.
Then,
Your power,
Your legacy,
Your centre will be no more.

Pause.

SPEAKERPHONE
GUARDS.
MOBILIZE AT THE FRONT GATES.
BREACH.

> *NEIKES hesitates.*
> *The window for escape is narrowing.*

TIRESIA
. . .
Go out the back way. Through my sanctuary.
They won't look for you there.

NEIKES
What?

TIRESIA
I won't stop you.
Go. Be safe.

> *Beat.*

I will take care of your ma.
I promise.
I promise.

> *Beat.*

Neikes. Your ma would be . . . so proud of you.
Now, go!

NEIKES
I . . .
Thank you.

TIRESIA gestures for NEIKES to move.
He nods at TIRESIA.
He grabs his umbrella,
Runs out.
The guards march in,
Grabbing the rest of the umbrellas.
TIRESIA points them in a different direction.
They leave.
TIRESIA is alone.

TIRESIA
Eunice,
Old friend.
I silenced you
So that I could have a voice.

I have kept you hidden
To spare your children
Pain.

But the ghosts of my guilt are waking:
Your son's truth
Swallows me whole.

I must fight
For your forgiveness.
Old friend.

Tonight,
At our sacred square,
Truth must spill.

She leaves.

SCENE 1.

The CHORUS enters
One by one,
Each clutching an umbrella,
Bright red like the folded sun.
They are split as if they were a
CHORUS of two opposing minds.
One half becomes CHORUS A (the military / opposing citizens),
And the other CHORUS B (the student protestors).
At various points, individual voices bubble up as well,
Signified with numbers (CHORUS A1, B2, etc.)

CHORUS B
We want freedom *(repeated)*

CHORUS A
Citizens.

                                          CHORUS B
                                          We are here.

CHORUS A
Citizens.

                                          CHORUS B
                                          We are here.

CHORUS A
Citizens.
STOP.
STOP THE MARCH.

CHORUS B
We do not fear you.
We will march
Till the square is ours.

CHORUS A
The square is not for you.
STOP THE MARCH.

Who leads you
In this mad mistake?

CHORUS B
Neikes!
Son of Kreon!
Neikes will avenge us all!

We see NEIKES *splinter*
From CHORUS B,
Facing CHORUS A *head-on.*

CHORUS A
Be warned.
You march at your own peril.

CHORUS B
We march for our own freedom!

We see TEO / CHORUS A1
Splinter from CHORUS A,
Approaching NEIKES.

TEO *throws up his hand,*
Ordering CHORUS A *to pause.*

TEO
Guards! Stop!
That's . . . that's my brother!

    Beat.

Let me reason with him.

          TEO runs to seize NEIKES.

          CHORUS B
          Who is that
          Boy
          Rushing towards us?

          NEIKES recognizes TEO and orders
          CHORUS B to stand down.

          NEIKES
          Teo!

TEO
Neikes!
What are you doing,
Leading this madness?
Why did you
Breach the centre?!

          NEIKES
          I *escaped*
          The centre.

TEO
ESCAPED?
How can you be so ungrateful
Towards your own re-education?!

> **NEIKES**
> Re-education is a lie, Teo!
> It's—

TEO
A lie?
It's a chance for redemption!
You threw away your life,
Your chance to follow in Pa's
Footsteps,
Leaving it all to me, *again*.
Why would you bring such shame
Onto our family?!

> **NEIKES**
> If you saw Ma,
> You'd understand true shame.

> *Beat.*

> Her mind's been wiped clean and empty.

> *Beat.*

> I couldn't bring her back . . .
> She was left behind with the others . . .

TEO
Ma belongs there!
The centre is for the troubled and lost,
That's what Pa / says!

> **NEIKES**
> The centre is not what he
> Says it is.
> Pa . . .

NEIKES corrects himself.

KREON is a traitor.

TEO
Pa is following the Supreme Leader's decree!
His word is sacred; he wouldn't lie to us!

NEIKES
The Supreme Leader is a piece of—

TEO
WATCH YOUR TONGUE, BROTHER.

Beat.

I-I don't believe you . . .

NEIKES
They tortured us, Teo!
They would make us—

TEO
The Supreme Leader is just.
He would never harm his own—

NEIKES
Believe me, Teo!
We're marching so that the world will know!

TEO
Your march is treason!

NEIKES
We march for justice.

Beat.

I'm doing this for MA, Teo!

TEO
The will of our Leader
Trumps
The will of all others,
Ma included.

NEIKES
If that's what you believe, brother,
Then live your wilful life
of willing blindness.

Beat.

Get out of my way.
Or else.

Beat.

Fine.
So be it.
The square will be ours.

TEO
If you march any farther,
I'll be forced to-to-to—

NEIKES
(to CHORUS B) THE SQUARE WILL BE OURS!

CHORUS B
THE SQUARE WILL BE OURS!

CHORUS B marches forwards.

NEIKES
We march
For FREEDOM.

TEO
YOUR MARCH LEADS US TO CHAOS.

NEIKES
(addressing CHORUS B) TO THE SQUARE.
Long live the people!

CHORUS B
(as they begin to march) Long live the people!
Long live the people!
Long live the people!

TEO
(addressing CHORUS A) Guards!
Prepare the barricade!

Suddenly
Both sides of the CHORUS converge.

SPEAKERPHONE
Citizens.
Martial law has been declared.

CHORUS B
Long live the people!

TEO
Detain those dogs,
Every single last one of them.

CHORUS B
Long live the—

They are kettled by CHORUS A.

CHORUS 2
What is going on?
They wouldn't harm us!
We are innocent!

SPEAKERPHONE
All protesters will be removed.
We advise all citizens to stay indoors at this time.

CHORUS 6
MOVE!

SPEAKERPHONE
Citizens.

CHORUS 2
We're not doing anything wrong.
We're just marching!
We just want—

SPEAKERPHONE
Stay inside. Stay inside.

CHORUS 2
We refuse to stay inside!
Long live the—

SPEAKERPHONE
Stay inside.

CHORUS 6
GET EVERY LAST ONE OF THOSE—

> **SPEAKERPHONE**
> Stay inside.

> **NEIKES**
> *(to CHORUS B)* Now,
> At the heels of the square,
> We demand justice for our disappeared.
> We demand that the Supreme Leader tells us the truth!
> And we want the world to witness us!
> Long live the people!
>
> *We hear a loud noise.*
> *A shot.*

> **CHORUS B**
> RUN. RUN.
> RUN!

> *Blackout.*
> *ANTIGONE screams.*

SCENE 2.

ANTIGONE
Ahhhhh!!

ISMENE
Are you all right?!

ANTIGONE
ISMENE!

ISMENE
What's— What's wrong?!

ANTIGONE
SISTER!

ISMENE
Antigone, it's okay, it's okay!
The power will be back, any sec.

ANTIGONE
ISMENE!

ISMENE
I'm here /
Shhh
I'm here . . .

ANTIGONE
Something's wrong at the square.
I think we—!

ISMENE
See?
Back to normal,
Nothing to be scared about!

ANTIGONE
Neikes is at the square!

ISMENE
W-what?
Calm down.
Neikes.
He's at the centre . . .
What do you mean?!

ANTIGONE
He must have escaped or /
I don't know . . .
All I know is he's back,
He's leading that march.

ISMENE
The march that Pa and Teo went to stop?

ANTIGONE
Yeah.

    Beat.

ISMENE
Oh my god . . .
Well . . .
The march will finish,
Then Pa, Teo, AND Neikes will come home!
They'll be fine!

                           ANTIGONE is silent.

What?

    Beat.

WHAT?!

    Beat.

ANTIGONE
They're clearing the square.
With force!

ISMENE
... With force?
What do you mean with—

    Beat.

Oh no.

ANTIGONE
What should we do?!
We ... we have to do something ...
COME WITH ME.
LET'S GO TO THE SQUARE.
It'll be safer together.

ISMENE
No
We can't
It's-it's—

ANTIGONE
Our family can be reunited tonight,
Let's go!

ISMENE
No no no no no,
We'll ... we'll wait for them here ...
In safety!
They wouldn't use force,
That's ridiculous!

ANTIGONE
I was listening in on the students' radio channel
There was some sort of ... of breach, or
I dunno,
Something at the centre,

Then
There was chanting,
Marching . . .
That's when I
I heard Neikes's voice,
Then a gunshot,
Then all of a sudden
Someone screamed
RUN. RUN. RUN
Then . . .
Silence.

    Beat.

We have to find them!

ISMENE
Are you out of your mind?
At what risk?!

ANTIGONE
What risk?!
Did you hear anything I said?
Our brothers are in danger!

ISMENE
Pa will find them.
It's his job; he's the friggin' chief.
We have to wait for him, at least!

ANTIGONE
I—we—have a responsibility for our family too.
We don't have time to wait for him!
Please, please, come with me,
Please!

ISMENE doesn't budge.

ISMENE
Antigone.
This is treason!

ANTIGONE
Your treason is
My reason.

ISMENE
It's a world of kings and men out there.
We're just two young girls.
That's why Teo and Pa told us to stay home,
They wanted us to be safe.
Stay with me. We'll hear from them soon,
I'm sure of it!

ANTIGONE
Ugh, coward!
THIS IS FAMILY.
Don't you care?!

ISMENE doesn't answer.

Fine.
Stay then.
I'll . . . I'll go alone.

    Beat.

I will find our scattered family.
You worry about your false safety.

ISMENE
Don't blame this on me.
Not all of us can disregard LAWS and LIVES like you.

    Beat.

Antigone.
We. Have. No. Power.

ANTIGONE
Then stay powerless, sister.

    Beat.

I'm going!

ISMENE
Don't be so rash!

ANTIGONE
I don't need your fear.
I need your courage!

ISMENE
Then—
Go quietly. Hidden.
Don't let them catch you, at least.

ANTIGONE
Oh no. no. not at all.
I will shout their names to the heavens,
Let it thunder through the clouds to find them,
At least.

ISMENE
Your passion scorches
All around you—

ANTIGONE
Your cowardice freezes
All around you—

ISMENE
Why are you always this
Impossible.

ANTIGONE
Because the possibility of seeing our family together
Is the greatest joy I can imagine.

> *ANTIGONE begins to leave.*

ISMENE
Don't be so stupid!

> *ANTIGONE is by the door.*

Antigone!
Wait!

> *ANTIGONE stops.*

I love you.

> *ANTIGONE begins to open the door,*
> *But just as she touches the doorknob,*
> *A desperate knock on the door.*
> *The sisters jump,*
> *Stare at each other.*

SCENE 3.

ISMENE
Get back!

ANTIGONE
It might be Pa!

ISMENE
Shhh.
(whispers) Get back!

> *ISMENE rushes to the door.*
> *ANTIGONE steps back,*
> *Huddles with ISMENE.*
>
> *Another knock. A voice emerges:*

HAEMON
. . . Is someone there?
. . . Hello?

> *ISMENE checks through the keyhole.*

ISMENE
(whispering) It's a man.
A student, I think—I don't know.
There's blood on him.

HAEMON
Please. Please help me.
Please . . . I have a message for . . .
Uh . . .

ISMENE
(whispering to ANTIGONE) What do we do?

ANTIGONE
Wait.

HAEMON
Please! I know you're in there.

>   *There is no answer.*

I know Neikes.
I was with him.
He told me to come here.

>   *ANTIGONE jumps to her feet.* ISMENE *follows, hesitantly.*

ANTIGONE
We have to—

ISMENE
We can't let him in.
He's one of the protestors!

ANTIGONE
We have to find out about our—

ISMENE
But—

ANTIGONE
Please.

ISMENE
Ugh, fine!
Once he's done talking
He has to go, okay!?

> ANTIGONE *hesitates,*
> *Then she nods yes.*

Let me handle this.

> *Beat.*

(through the door) Were you being followed?

HAEMON
Oh thank god. Um,
No. I'm alone.

ISMENE
What do you have to say to us?

HAEMON
I . . . well . . .
Please, it's not safe for me out here.
Please, I'll tell you, just let me in.

ISMENE
(considers for a moment, then whispers) Stand over there.
Grab something just in case.

> ANTIGONE *grabs an umbrella by the door.*

Ready?

ANTIGONE nods.

ISMENE
(through the door) We're going to open the doors.
Put your hands behind your head.

ANTIGONE
What are you doing?

ISMENE
Just to be safe.
(through the door) Now turn around.

She checks through the door.
She opens it swiftly,
Expertly holds his hands down, and pulls him into the home.

HAEMON
Whoa stop stop stop, my arm—my arm!

ISMENE
Get down.

She subdues him on the ground.
ANTIGONE drops the umbrella to help ISMENE.

ANTIGONE
Ismene. Whoa.

HAEMON
Ow ow! Stop!

ISMENE
Who are you?!

HAEMON
Haemon!—
Ow, ow.

ISMENE
You were with Neikes?

ANTIGONE
Where is he?!

HAEMON
I—uh, I don't know.
I was with him
At the re-education centre.
I—ow!
Please, let go of me.

ISMENE
Keep your hands behind your head.

HAEMON
I—my shoulder—

ISMENE
What?

HAEMON
It's, it's still . . .

    Beat.

        ISMENE notices the blood on her hands for the first time.
            She immediately lets go of HAEMON.

ISMENE
Oh my god,
I am so sorry.

HAEMON
It's fine, I understand.
Neikes said you were . . . disciplined
. . . But he didn't mention your . . . uh . . . your . . .

He implies their military training through a gesture.

ISMENE & ANTIGONE
Our pa's a cop.

Beat.

HAEMON
Can you please um . . .
Do you have a towel or some gauze or . . . anything
For the . . . *(gestures to the wound)*

ISMENE
Oh, of course.

Beat.

Use this for now.
I'll go get a . . .

        ISMENE *chucks a shirt at* ANTIGONE, *makes for the exit.*

(to ANTIGONE*)* You got this?

ANTIGONE
Yea.

> *ISMENE goes.*
> *ANTIGONE chucks the shirt to HAEMON.*

HAEMON
(shyly) I—I
I need some help . . .

ANTIGONE
Oh.
Um. Okay.

> *ANTIGONE hesitantly approaches HAEMON's shoulder,*
> *Winces at the blood.*

HAEMON
Thank you.

ANTIGONE
I can't get to the uh . . . the wound.
Can you—can you lift your um . . .
Can you lift your shirt a little?

HAEMON
Uh . . .

ANTIGONE
Or, here, I'll just—

> *ANTIGONE reaches through the neck of his shirt and dabs the blood.*
> *They share a moment of tender, awkward silence.*

. . . So . . . you were saying . . .

HAEMON
Yes. I need to . . . uh . . .

Beat.

Neikes sent me to find Kreon.

ANTIGONE
He sent you to find Pa?
Why?
What happened?

> *As* HAEMON *begins describing the events of the protest,*
> *The* CHORUS *begins to reassemble itself.*

HAEMON
We were at the front of the march.
I was just a little behind Neikes, holding banners,
When your other brother, Teo, ran up to stop us.
Neikes persisted, and we began to march towards the square . . .

SCENE 4.

> *We flash back to the protest at the square.*
> *The* CHORUS *awakens as student protestors.*

HAEMON
We were ten thousand strong.

> **CHORUS**
> Long live the people!
> Long live the people!
> Long live the people!
> WE WANT OUR GLORIOUS WORLD BACK!

HAEMON
We were a sea of red and gold.

CHORUS
The whole world is watching.
The whole world is watching.
The whole world is watching.

HAEMON
As we closed
Upon the square . . .

CHORUS
A speech! A speech!
Neikes is making a speech!

NEIKES
Brothers and sisters,
We are standing here at the Square of the People
Demanding truth and justice over our
Re-education system!

Witness us!

For a decade
I could do nothing but wish upon my ma's fate.
I could do nothing but ask over and over again,
"Where did she go?"
"What happened to her?!"

All I ever heard back was,
"She is being 're-educated.'"

So I did what I had to, to find my ma.

I exiled myself to the centre
Under the guise of being a thief,
A good-for-nothing,

A soul in need of
Re-education.

When I finally found her at the centre,
She . . . she was a
Ghost in a shell,
Surviving the isolation chambers
That eat up your waking moments there.

I am here to redeem her
And ALL the forgotten
Left to rot at the centre
By our supreme coward of a Leader.

Give them back their lives,
Give us back our freedoms.
You cannot disappear us.

We demand that he release
ALL the re-educated!

Beat.

Long live the people!

CHORUS
Long live the people!

A gunshot rings out through the crowds.

CHORUS (ONE MEMBER)
RUN. RUN. RUN!

Their umbrellas are held tight, like a weapon or shield.

The umbrellas stomp the earth
As they all stumble into chaos.
They build and build as this speech runs on.

HAEMON
Everyone just started
Sprinting, screaming, pushing
Their way backwards,
Friend's feet on friend's faces.
An ocean of people toppling over one another.

I—
I started running,
Making my way against the crowd,
But
Some man runs into me,
Pushes me over,
Steps on my shoulder.
His heels
Dig into my flesh.
Another woman steps on my hand.
I scream:
I'M ALIVE, I'M ALIVE
STOP STEPPING ON ME,
I'M ALIVE.

All of a sudden—

NEIKES
Run.
Go to my sisters
Antigone and Ismene.
Find them.
Tell them about Ma.
About the centre.

Tell them the truth.
Then.
Get a hold of Kreon.

HAEMON does not move.

You know what you have to do!
GO!

HAEMON
What?! No! Don't go, Neikes.

NEIKES
I have to find Teo.

But they're shooting!

NEIKES
RUN!

He pushes HAEMON with the crowd, and NEIKES runs the other way.

Back in the present with ANTIGONE:

HAEMON
I'm sorry that I lost him.
I came straight here to tell you.

ANTIGONE
I have to go to the square.

HAEMON
No. It's too dangerous.

ANTIGONE
I need to find—

HAEMON
They shot at everyone.
Your brother, Teo, shot at us too!
There are bodies everywhere.
How are you going to find Neikes?

ANTIGONE
I will.
I-I just will.

HAEMON
Help me find Kreon.
He can stop this.

ANTIGONE
If Pa finds you, if he knows you're here,
You're done for.

>   *Beat.*

You need to leave.

HAEMON
I need to find Kreon /
Ow.

>   *HAEMON winces from pain.*
>   *ANTIGONE checks the bloodied shirt. The bleeding has slowed.*

ANTIGONE
The bleeding, it—

HAEMON
It's fine, thank you—

>   *ISMENE charges in clutching rubbing alcohol and some gauze.*

ISMENE
(as she's entering) Um, this is all I could find /
. . . Antigone?!

ISMENE rushes to defend ANTIGONE.

ANTIGONE
I—we—were just talking—

ISMENE
Just talking?—

HAEMON
Yep. Just talking—

ANTIGONE
Haemon was at the centre.
He was at the front lines in the square!

ISMENE
He's one of *them!*—

HAEMON
You don't know what they did to us at the centre!

ISMENE
And I don't want to know.
Can't trust you.

ANTIGONE
Ismene, please,
He knows about Ma!

ISMENE
Ma?
How is she?

HAEMON
She's . . .
Well . . .

ANTIGONE
She's been
Re-educated.

ISMENE
Oh,
She must be well then.
Can she come home now?

HAEMON
She won't. Can't.

ISMENE
Why?

HAEMON
Re-education is a lie.
As a student
They would starve us,
They would make us kneel,
Arms outstretched,
For hours on end . . .

　　Beat.

For the elders,
The ones closer to "re-education,"
They were kept alone for days,
Months,
Years,
And your ma . . .
She wouldn't be able to recognize either of you.

ISMENE
You're lying!
The re-education centre is for glorious redemption,
We all know that.

Beat.

You've said what you needed,
Now leave!

ANTIGONE
They shot the students at
The square!
Our brothers are still out there,
And Haemon could help us find them!

Beat.

ISMENE
Was Pa there?!

SCENE 5.

*KREON appears at the door and
Knocks on it.
Beat.
ISMENE, ANTIGONE, and HAEMON look at each other,
Unsure of how to proceed.*

ISMENE
Oh my god oh my god oh my god . . .

ANTIGONE
Calm down!

ISMENE
Oh my god!
We have *this* traitor with us!

ANTIGONE
Shh!
It could just be the—

Knock knock.

KREON
Antigone. Ismene.
Open the door—

ANTIGONE
Never mind—

ISMENE
Oh my god oh my god . . .

HAEMON
What?

ISMENE & ANTIGONE
It's Pa.

ISMENE
We're screwed.

ANTIGONE
Ismene.
Stall.

   Beat.

I'll take him to the basement.

> ISMENE *rushes to the door.*

ISMENE
YOU WANT TO HIDE HIM?!

ANTIGONE
Shhhh!

ISMENE
(whispers) The basement?!

ANTIGONE
Trust me! Just stall.

ISMENE
(whispers) Oh no oh no . . .
This is real bad.

    Beat.

ANTIGONE
The blood!
Get the blood off your hands.

> ANTIGONE *gathers the gauze, alcohol, and shirt,*
> *Helps* HAEMON *to his feet.*
> *They make their way to the basement. Slowly.*
> ISMENE *stalls desperately.*

ISMENE
Who is it?! Just a sec!

> *The keys rattle impatiently in the lock.*

KREON
Ismene?

ISMENE
PA!
Um.
Hold on.

KREON
Open the door.

> *He knocks louder.*
> *The key clicks.*
> KREON *nudges the door open.*
> ISMENE *resists.*

ISMENE
Just. One. Second.

KREON
Open. The. Door.

> ANTIGONE *and* HAEMON *exit.*

ISMENE
GOT IT!

> ISMENE *jumps out of the way.*
> KREON *enters.*

KREON
Ismene.

ISMENE
Pa.

> *She bows to him. A deep bow from the hip,*
> *A sign of respect / filial piety to one's parents.*

Oh, forgetting your keys again?

KREON
Where's Antigone?

ISMENE
. . .
Bathroom.

KREON
(calls through the house) Antigone!

ISMENE
Are you thirsty?
Are you hungry?
Pa, sit down, the square must have been . . .
Madness.
Sit,
I'll get you a—

KREON
Can't sit.
Get your sister.

ISMENE
She's—she's
In the bathroom.
Upset stomach.
Can't rush an upset stomach.
I'll get you that—

KREON stares.

ANTIGONE enters, rubbing her hands.
ISMENE sighs in relief.

Beat.

ANTIGONE
Pa!

ANTIGONE *bows.*

KREON
Antigone.

ANTIGONE
How's the square?

KREON
. . .

Beat.

ANTIGONE
How are you?

KREON
Fine.
You?

Beat.

ANTIGONE
Scared.

Pause.

KREON
Me too.

They sit in silence for a bit.
ISMENE *enters with water.*

ISMENE
Pa.

KREON
Sit down.

They do.

I— I have some news.
Well, first
I am happy to say
The . . . the . . . *riots* at the
Square
Have been crushed.
The *rioters* have been
Taken care of.
We are safe.

ANTIGONE
What / happened?

KREON
Don't interrupt.

Beat.

There is still much to be done.
I have to go back,
Shortly.

Beat.

But before that . . .
I have come
To ask for your support,
In the way that the both of you
Stood by me
When . . . when Ma . . .
Was sent for re-education.

> ISMENE *and* ANTIGONE *look at each other, doubtful.*

(*searches for words*) I am proud to say:
That . . .
I have been tasked with
Clearing our square.

ANTIGONE
Of what?

KREON
Of
Garbage.

ISMENE
Garbage?

ANTIGONE
Pa?

KREON
(*as if this has been prepared*) It is impossible to judge a man
Until you've seen them lead.
Lead a business,
Lead a country,
Lead a *march.*

Only in leading
Can you see what cloth a man is cut from.
What passions stir his actions,
What agendas boil underneath,
What allegiances he holds.
If this man
Values any,
And I mean anything,
Above the motherland,
Then they are . . .
Well, I don't count them
Men.

    Beat.

I thought I raised two excellent sons.
But I failed.
One of them breached the centre
And led the march.
He's *garbage.*

               We see NEIKES *and* TEO, *a flashback of their fate,*
               With their umbrellas,
               Circling each other in the middle of the square.
               They run at each other,
               And as they meet
               Their umbrellas bloom,
               Revealing swathes of red.
               They fall.

               We see KREON *change this narrative in telling*
               His daughters.

A son that dishonours my legacy,
OUR family,
Is no son at all.

We will relinquish him
From our blood.
We will erase all pictures of him.
The mention of his name will be met with imprisonment.
This is our Leader's decree.
We must obey, daughters.
This is law.

We cannot let one rotten son
Ruin the order I've forged for us,
For our city.

    Beat.

You should have seen the way my own men
Were looking at me . . . the disgrace, the dishonour,
The disgust.

    Beat.

The Supreme Leader has led us through a thousand years
Of sweeping glory.
And tonight
He has given me
The honour of proving my loyalty.
So . . .
I will clear the square.

I'm doing this for us,
Daughters.
This is how we survive.

    Beat.

Stand by me.

Long pause.

ISMENE
I'm sorry, Pa.

ANTIGONE
(sharply) For what?

ISMENE
I'm sorry for your hurt.

ISMENE holds KREON's hands.

Beat.

ANTIGONE
Is he dead?

KREON
What?

ANTIGONE
Is Neikes dead?

KREON
Does it matter?

ANTIGONE
Is he?!

KREON does not respond.

ISMENE
(hushed) How about Teo . . .
He's fine, right, Pa?
He's safe?

KREON
Teo is . . .
An honourable son.

    Beat.

He was caught in the stampede,
I could only recognize him
From his uniform and badge
He . . .

    Beat.

Teo will receive
The most distinguished burial
In our lands.
While the rest of the waste will be cleared
Into a landfill and left to
Rot . . .
Anyone who touches their bodies will
Be executed.

    Beat.

Teo is . . .
He was a good son.

               ISMENE sobs.
        ANTIGONE hugs her and cries too.
    KREON stands next to the two girls,
          Unsure of how to comfort them.
 He places his hands on their shoulders and lowers his head.

SCENE 6.

A knock on the door. A sort of comical knock,
A casual knock that disarms.

KREON
It's for me.

KREON heads for the door. Checks.
Opens the door.
GUARD is standing there, looking like they're going to pee themselves.
They speak fast as lightning, slowing to make a
Point or when they recoil.

Yes?

GUARD
Sir,
(sees ANTIGONE and ISMENE) Ma'am—
I mean, mademoiselles
I mean, missus, er, misses.
Ahh, they sound the same.
Um
Miss and miss.

Beat.

Good evening.

KREON glares.

Um.
Can I—
I mean, may I
Come in?

KREON
No—

GUARD
Oh—

KREON
Speak—

GUARD
I'm sorry I took so
Um long.
I got a little lost around all these . . .
I mean . . .
Wow!
All these huge houses:
You can basically have a factory in your
Basement!
I mean, look at the size of of
Of this,
Um . . .

So yea, I got a little lost.
And no lies,
I was gonna maybe turn around,
Stop for a snack or two,
Just telling myself:
Man, you're so screwed,
You're so done.
What an epic fail.

KREON
Get to it.

GUARD
Sooooooo . . .
You know how uh
We were keeping the live ones . . .
From . . . phase one?

Realizes that ANTIGONE *and* ISMENE *are listening intently.*

Did I just say PHASE ONE?

Beat.

Oh god, I just said it again.

KREON
(sighs) They're my daughters.
It's fine.

Not quite understanding the point.

GUARD
Uh . . . okay.
So.
The sheep in this ONE farm,
Well,
We did a roll call, like, a who's here kinda thing,
And uh,
One of the *more* important sheep . . .
Well. *It* was missing.
So.

KREON
Which one?

GUARD
Uh *it* has brown hair? Kinda angry looking.

KREON
Name.

GUARD
Um
It's name
Is . . .
Are you sure I should say it in front of the girls?

KREON
Talk, or I'll take your tongue.

GUARD
Whoa. Okay.
Um.
Haemon Ahn.
We couldn't locate him.

> *A bump from the basement.*
> ISMENE *looks at* ANTIGONE.
> ANTIGONE *gestures to keep quiet.*

Beat.

Oh god, please don't punish me.
Me and the other guards had to pull sticks to decide
Who'd come and tell you . . .
And lucky guess!
It's me! *ALWAYS* me.
Um
Please.

KREON
. . . Check the bodies.
He might be there.

GUARD
Um no.
We saw him run off.
He was injured and bleeding, but he weaseled into some alleyways
And escaped.

    Beat.

Honestly,
He outran us.

    Beat.

Please have mercy.

                ANTIGONE *and* ISMENE *hold each other's hands.*

KREON
Fool!
This is what you will do—
Reinforce the perimeters,
Broadcast his name,
Set a bounty
For five million.

    Beat.

We'll find him within the hour.

                We hear another small bump from the basement.

GUARD
Should we continue on then . . .
Should we begin . . . phase two?

KREON
Go.
I'll be right behind you.

GUARD
. . . Is that a yes? / Or . . . a . . .

KREON
GO!

GUARD
Yes, sir!
I promise I won't fail!
Looking for the boy, I mean.
And, well, based on this, it's not looking so hot.
But!
Here's to second chances!
Thanks, sir,
And, um,
Miss and miss.

> *GUARD bows and leaves.*
> *KREON gathers his things, getting ready to leave.*

KREON
Do either of you know this
Haemon Ahn?

ISMENE & ANTIGONE
Nope. Nope.

> *Another bump in the basement.*

KREON
. . . What's that noise?

ISMENE & ANTIGONE
Um . . .

Beat.

ANTIGONE
. . . This is so embarrassing but um . . .
I— I might have clogged the bathroom.

ISMENE
Upset stomach.
See, shouldn't rush an upset stomach.

ANTIGONE
Yup. Yup.
I'll— I'll go take care of it.

Beat.

KREON
This Haemon Ahn . . .
He's one of the other student leaders that escaped the centre.
A fellow *traitor* along with the rest of the *waste*.
Keep vigilant.

Beat.

I'm going.
I have your support,
Yes?

ISMENE
Yes, Pa.

KREON
Antigone?

ANTIGONE
I— I . . .

KREON
He is not your brother anymore,
Not my son,
Not our family.
He's
Garbage.

    Beat.

We will mourn for Teo properly
After all of this is over . . .

    Beat.

Our strength comes from swallowing—

                    ANTIGONE *reacts to the word swallowing.*

Surpassing our shame.
Remember this.

    Beat.

Do you understand, Antigone?

ANTIGONE
I . . .
I do.

KREON
. . .
Stay here.
Do not leave the house.

Beat.

Tomorrow we begin forgetting this shame.
As for tonight . . .
May heaven have mercy.

KREON leaves.

SCENE 7.

ISMENE and ANTIGONE look at each other.
They feel such relief.

ISMENE
Oh my god oh my god oh my god.
What are we going to do about Haemon?!

ANTIGONE
Help him escape.

ISMENE
WHAT?
HE'S A WANTED MAN.
We should have given him over right then and there!

ANTIGONE
And why didn't you?

ISMENE
I-I-I—
Well, Pa would be—

ANTIGONE
You're a coward.

ISMENE
NO!
I didn't want us to get in trouble, that's it!

>   *Beat.*

We can't side with him!
Think of Pa!
Think of our future!
If anyone were to find out, we'd be—
Pa would be—

>   *Beat.*

We have to turn him in.

ANTIGONE
Sure, you turn him in,
You hand him over to Pa,
Then what?

What happens when Pa finds out
That we hid him, that we dressed his wounds?
That we helped him?

ISMENE
Oh my god oh my god . . .

>   *Beat.*

We are so screwed.

ANTIGONE
He doesn't have to find out.

ISMENE
What?

ANTIGONE
We'll help Haemon run.
Sneak him past the city perimeters
As soon as we can.
Then . . . he's on his own.

    Beat.

If you do this, Pa will never find out,
And we'll be in the clear.

ISMENE
. . .
We—
We don't even know him.
We can't trust him!

ANTIGONE
Neikes did.

ISMENE
And look what happened to him!
Our brother is a shame to us.

ANTIGONE
Neikes is still our brother.

ISMENE
And so is Teo!

ANTIGONE
Then do it for me, Ismene.
Blood is blood.

If we cannot mourn for Neikes,
The least we can do is help his friend.
He wanted Haemon to go free,
That is that.

    Beat.

Can you do this?

ISMENE
... I mean ...
FINE.
YOU do it.
You help him.
I'll just ...
I'll keep my mouth shut.

    Beat.

ANTIGONE
Thank you.

ISMENE
But he leaves tonight.

                    ISMENE makes to go.

    Beat.

                    ISMENE goes for the basement.

ANTIGONE
Wait.

                    ISMENE stops.

Ismene,
I'm going to, uh
Will you, uh . . .
Will you . . .

ISMENE
What?

ANTIGONE
Never mind.
I just wanted to say . . .
I love you.

ISMENE
Yea yea,
Whatever.
UGH
I can't believe I'm
Helping you!

ISMENE leaves.

ANTIGONE looks around,
Grabs the black umbrella,
Makes for the door.
ANTIGONE leaves.

After a little time, ISMENE re-enters with HAEMON.

You nearly got us caught.
What the hell was with all the—

HAEMON
I'm sorry, was just trying to hear the—

ISMENE
You were eavesdropping?!
For shame!
God, if Pa had found out you were here . . .

HAEMON
I—thank you.
Thank you for—

ISMENE
Oh stop it,
I don't want to help you . . . just—

>   *Beat.*

Antigone!

HAEMON
Where is—

ISMENE
She's probably gone to pack you some clothes.
I'll throw in some gauze and whatnot,
And she'll sneak you to the perimeters . . .
And you'll have to . . .
You'll have to run or hide or . . .
I don't know.

HAEMON
I-I can't go back out there.

ISMENE
And you can't stay here.
So.

Beat.

(calling out) ANTIGONE.

> HAEMON *notices the missing umbrella.*

HAEMON
Wait.

ISMENE
What?

HAEMON
Her umbrella . . .
It's . . .

> HAEMON *gestures over*
> *To the missing umbrella.*
> ISMENE *looks . . . nothing.*

ISMENE
Oh my god.
She told me to help you!
She said she'd lead you to the perimeters!
Why would she just . . .

HAEMON
What?

ISMENE
She's . . . going to the square.
She must be.

HAEMON
What?

ISMENE
She's going to find Neikes's body.

    Beat.

The guard said that they were about to begin . . .

HAEMON
Phase two.

ISMENE
Yea.

                                        Pause.

HAEMON
I can get us through the . . .

ISMENE
I don't trust you.

HAEMON
I mean you no harm.
Believe me.

ISMENE
I don't.

    Beat.

HAEMON
What are you going to do?

SCENE 8.

We are thrust into the greater world.
The space clears from an interior location and expands and grows
Splinter by splinter
Into the square.

ANTIGONE appears stage right.
She runs around the stage,
Ducking in and out of cover.

As she is running
We hear the speakerphones spliced with individual
CHORUS members present at the square:

SPEAKERPHONE
Citizens.
Martial law has been declared.
Phase two is about to begin.
Leave the square.
Do not touch the bodies
Or you will be executed.
They are to be removed tonight.

CHORUS 4
I was just walking through the square.
I was just walking.
I was just walking.
Why am I being detained?
Why am I under arrest?
I was just passing through, honest!
I promise, I'm not,
I'm not a protestor.
I-I don't have an umbrella or a tag.
I don't know their chants,

Their slogans.
I'm NOT a protestor.
LET GO OF ME.
WHY ARE YOU TAKING ME AWAY?

SPEAKERPHONE
All revolutionaries have been detained.

CHORUS 1
(injured) Run. Run. Run.
Run from the square.
Run from the law.
Run for your life.

SPEAKERPHONE
All rioters have been removed.

CHORUS (ALL)
(punctuating the shift) MOVE—

CHORUS 5
Move along!
You're blocking the friggin' road.
Gotta drive my grandma to the hospital.
Go! Get outta the way!
You idiots
Got nothing better to do than
Hang around the street
Chanting your little slogans—

SPEAKERPHONE
All protesters have been arrested.

CHORUS 3
That's my SON.
LET HIM GO.

He's not a rioter—he's not! Let him go!
I don't care if you're the police,
The Supreme Leader.
I don't care if you're the friggin lord above.
THAT IS MY SON.
HE'S NOT A RIOTER.
LET HIM GO.
YOU CAN'T JUST DISAPPEAR
MY SON.

SPEAKERPHONE
Phase two is about to begin.

CHORUS 7
Freedom!
We want freedom!
We want freedom!

CHORUS 6
Whose freedom?
Do you even know what you're
Fighting for?

Beat.

Just leave it be.
What's all the fuss about?
You got food,
You got houses,
You got families.

Beat.

Ungrateful dogs.

CHORUS 1
Run. Run. Run.
They're back.
Out to clear the square.
RUN before they run you down!

SPEAKERPHONE
We advise you to stay indoors at this time.
Leave the bodies. Do not touch them.

CHORUS 3
I am not leaving the square until you
Bring me my son.

Until you bring back
Our children—

CHORUS 4
Our parents—

CHORUS 5
Our loved ones—

CHORUS 6
Our enemies—

CHORUS 1
Our friends—

CHORUS 7
Our teachers—

CHORUS (ALL)
Our peace,
Our city.

> We will not stay indoors
> While our hearts are beating in the square.

SPEAKERPHONE
Leave the bodies—

> CHORUS 3
> I am not leaving until—

SPEAKERPHONE
Leave the square—

> CHORUS 1
> I won't run.
> I won't leave.
> LONG LIVE THE PEOPLE.

SPEAKERPHONE
Leave the square—

> CHORUS 3
> Do you have a child?
> A son?
> Would you ever,
> Ever leave him behind?
> Exactly.
> I am not leaving until you tell me where he is.

SPEAKERPHONE
YOU HAVE BEEN WARNED.

> CHORUS 5
> Oh frig.
> But GRANNY HAS TO GET TO THE HOSPITAL.
> We can't go home NOW.

You friggin' idiot students clogging the streets!
MY GRANNY HAS TO—

SPEAKERPHONE
YOU HAVE BEEN WARNED.

> *Phase two begins.*
> *A giant cloud of white smoke is blown into the square:*
> *Tear gas.*
> *The* CHORUS *shields themselves with umbrellas,*
> *Covering their mouths,*
> *Coughing,*
> *Buckling under the assault.*

Leave.

> **CHORUS**
> If leaving is to live:
> We choose to
> Stay and die.

SPEAKERPHONE
Your choice.

> *The tear gas is thrown again.*
> *The* CHORUS *gets knocked down to their knees.*
> *The* CHORUS *is buffeted with white smoke.*
> *They fall.*

Phase two has begun.
The square is to be cleared shortly.
We advise you to stay indoors at this time.
Stay inside.
Stay inside.
Stay inside.

Stay—
Bzzzzzzzzz

SCENE 9. THE ODE.

The square swells with conflict,
But for a dreamlike second
The CHORUS speaks:

Note: this can be performed solo, by CHORUS 4,
Or can be performed chorally, with each member of the chorus
(Minus ANTIGONE or the GUARD / CHORUS 5)
Taking one line at a time.

CHORUS
How strange is the world
How confusing
How clear
How incredible
How disappointing
How angry
How funny
How utterly strange is our world

But compared to mankind . . .
Well,
The world sits back to
How confusing
How clear
How incredible
How disappointing
How angry
How funny
How utterly strange we humans are

We fly through the skies
Sail through the seas
Conquer our lands
Inch by inch
As if the world belongs to us alone

The winged creatures that share our skies
We shoot them down and scream
THE SKY IS OURS

The fanged beasts that share our earth
We trap them and scream
THE LAND IS OURS

The fish, the sharks, the submerged entities
We take our nets, our knives, and scream
YOUR FLESH IS OURS

We, men, masters of animals
Of cities
Of countries
Of each other
Whipping through our tongues
Speaking like thunder to show just how smart we are
Flaunting our hair
Brushing our faces to show just how beautiful we are
We answer every unknown with an arrogance of
We know it all, we know it all
We know everything

But
Do we?
What happens afterwards?
After the fall?
After we disappear?

What happens when we die?

We vibrate between the law and our lives
Between being good and being bad
If man veers and stays with the good
Well
Good for him
But if man derails
Finds himself warping his tongue
Into bitterness and anger
Finds himself disappearing others
For the sake of his own appearances
Finds himself
A leader, leading us to the end instead of the light
If man stays with evil
Well
Good for him
He proves just how utterly strange we are

SCENE 10.

> As the CHORUS finishes "The Ode,"
> We see ANTIGONE slipping through the perimeter.
> She is hiding her face and hunched over
> Lying low on the ground,
> Covering her face from the tear gas.

> We watch ANTIGONE crawl through the umbrella wasteland
> Slowly as she pants / grunts / forces her way through the ruins.

ANTIGONE
(crawling through the umbrellas) Neikes!

CHORUS 1
Who is that girl?

CHORUS 7
O that poor child!
Did she not hear the orders?!
Does she not fear the gas?
What is she looking for?

CHORUS 4
She should be running away
From the square,
Not towards it.

> *ANTIGONE rummages through the umbrellas*
> *But patiently, honourably, picks each up*
> *And lets them fall with grace and respect.*
> *She grows increasingly urgent as she searches*
> *And searches*
> *And searches.*

ANTIGONE
Neikes!!!

> *Then finally*
> *She spots*
> *NEIKES.*

Oh!

> *ANTIGONE wails to the heavens.*
>
> *She hugs his body tight*
> *As she slowly, slowly composes herself.*

> *She begins to stand,*
> *Lifts* NEIKES *over her back*
> *(This takes much effort).*
> *She cannot.*
> *She fumbles.*
> *She falls.*
> *But tries and tries again.*
> *She finally finds a way to hoist his body*
> *Over her shoulders.*
> *She begins to leave the square,*
> *But her steps are slow and solemn*

>   ANTIGONE
> *Crosses the square*
> *With her brother on her back.*

SCENE 11.

>   *Suddenly*
> *The* GUARD *sees her,*
> *Calls out:*

GUARD
STOP, MISSY. STOP.

> *The* GUARD *runs towards her.*
> ANTIGONE *keeps walking.*

STOP RIGHT THERE.

> *The* GUARD *blocks her path.*

ANTIGONE
. . . Get out of my way.

GUARD
Or what?
What the hell do you think you're doing?

ANTIGONE
I am bringing him home.

GUARD
Uh, no you aren't.
Didn't you hear?
DO NOT TOUCH THE BODIES.
You're breaking the law, missy!

ANTIGONE
Your law, not mine.
Now get out of my way.

ANTIGONE takes a step forward.

GUARD
Whoa now. Calm down.
Leave that body here with me
And I'll pretend like I never saw you,
How's that sound?
Less trouble for the both of us.

ANTIGONE
This is my brother.
I will not leave him to rot.

GUARD
That's . . .

Beat.

Kreon's son . . . !

Beat.

You're . . .
Does your pa know you're here?!
Miss, no no no,
You, you have to go now.
The disgrace you will bring on Kreon if
If if . . . miss, you have to leave the body here!

ANTIGONE
LEAVE ME ALONE.
MOVE.
GET AWAY.

> *The* GUARD *readies his weapon.*

GUARD
Don't move!

> *ANTIGONE stands defiant.*
> *The* GUARD *steps forward.*

> *ISMENE and HAEMON*
> *Are seen running through the square.*
> *They are keeping low to the ground,*
> *Making their way to the centre of the square.*

Miss.
The gas is cleared.
Soon the bulldozers will
Come through
To sweep the square.
You have to go now.

Leave him here with me,
And I'll never tell Kreon,
Promise.

ANTIGONE
Tell Kreon.
He should see his son.
He deserves to see what he's
Clearing.

SCENE 12.

> ISMENE *and* HAEMON
> *Spot* ANTIGONE *through the dwindling fog.*

ISMENE & HAEMON
Antigone!

ANTIGONE
(under her breath) No.

> *They rush to stand between* ANTIGONE *and the* GUARD.

ISMENE
Why did you run off like that?!

ANTIGONE
Why did you follow me?!

ISMENE
I couldn't leave you alone!
We sneaked through the perimeter

Chasing after you—
You friggin' fool.
I love you, but GOD you're such a—

> *ISMENE sees NEIKES.*

... Is that ... ?

> *ANTIGONE lets go of her brother's body for*
> *ISMENE to see.*

Neikes ...

> *Beat.*

Oh. My. God.

GUARD
Other miss?!
Who's this boy ...
Aren't you ...

> *The GUARD realizes that this is HAEMON.*
> *HAEMON stands his ground.*

YOU'RE THE BOY
The one that escaped!

> *Beat.*

I caught him! YES!
I did it!
Phewwwwwww.

> *Beat.*

HAEMON AHN.

ANTIGONE
Haemon! Run!

HAEMON doesn't budge.

GUARD
Nuh uh. Don't you dare.
I've caught you, BOY.
Keep your hands in the air!
(speaking to CHORUS) Go get Kreon.
WOOHOOOO. TELL HIM
THAT I CAUGHT HIM.
He'll get a good laugh outta that!
Can't believe my luck.
Two birds with one—
Well, I guess, more like,
Three birds with one stone!

The GUARD makes his way, weapons raised, towards HAEMON.

(suddenly serious) Kreon will be so
Pleased
To see you.

SCENE 13.

> *KREON enters.*
> *ANTIGONE and ISMENE are watching by NEIKES's body.*
> *HAEMON is standing tall.*

GUARD
Sir.

> *The GUARD bows.*

KREON
Antigone. Ismene.
Why are you here?!
Who's this?

GUARD
Well, I mean,
I didn't expect to,
To, you know,
Come back to you with any sort of
Good news or
Any news at all, for that matter . . .
But. Hey!
It's my lucky day!
I found Haemon!
Five million is the reward, yea?

KREON
Out of my way.

> *Beat.*

This is the boy?

GUARD
Yup. Yep.
Take him.
Do what you want with him.
Disappear him.
I was totally joking about the money . . .

   Beat.

FOR THE MOTHERLAND.

What should I do with him, sir?

KREON
Let me handle it.

                           KREON approaches HAEMON.

(to HAEMON) You left your family at the *centre*,
You selfish *boy*.
You are a disgrace to them,
And to us all.

   Beat.

You will never see them again.
(to his daughters) Why were you with this traitor?
Why are you here?

ISMENE
Pa, he . . .
He was just helping us!

KREON
Helping you?

Pause.

ISMENE
. . . Antigone.
I-I have to tell the—

ANTIGONE
Don't say it—

ISMENE
We have to tell the truth.
It's the only way out of this . . .

KREON
Speak!

ISMENE
Pa.

   Beat.

I share the blame.
Antigone and I . . .

We hid Haemon.
We took care of him.
We helped him.
He was the last to see . . .
And and
We wanted to find our brother so . . .
We didn't mean to hurt you like this.
I-I'm sorry.
WE'RE sorry, right . . . Antigone?

ANTIGONE
You've done it, Ismene . . .

Pause.

KREON
You. Hid. The boy.
And helped him?!
When I had asked for you to stay vigilant.

> *For the slightest second, as* KREON *is speaking to*
> ANTIGONE *and* ISMENE,
> *His back is turned to* HAEMON.
> *Like coiled lightning,*
> HAEMON *whips out a dagger.*

HAEMON
AHHHHHH!

> HAEMON *charges at* KREON.

GUARD
Sir!
Look out!—

> *The* GUARD, *delayed,*
> *Draws his weapon.*

ANTIGONE
Haemon!—

ISMENE
Pa!—

> HAEMON *closes upon* KREON,
> *But with lighting-quick reflexes,*
> ISMENE *expertly deflects his attack,*
> *Shoulder locks him onto the ground, and disarms him.*
> HAEMON *is on the ground yelling.*

HAEMON
IT'S ALL YOUR FAULT, KREON—

GUARD
Get out of the way, miss!
I-I can't aim with—

HAEMON
THIS IS FOR NEIKES—
LET ME GO.

ISMENE
You—

HAEMON
LET ME GO!
This man . . . this man,
He sent my family to the centre!

ISMENE
Stop struggling!

HAEMON
I BLAME EVERYTHING ON YOU,
KREON.
WE WERE A POOR FAMILY.
We needed to eat!
The state rations weren't enough to feed us all.
We—we needed to survive,
So we grew our own food,
Against HIS GLORIOUS DECREE.
We weren't harming anybody!
We didn't deserve to be sent to the centre!
My ma and pa disintegrated within a month
Of being there!
I had no one.

I was kept in isolation.
I was-was losing my frigging MIND
Until
Neikes / freed us—

KREON
Don't say his name!

HAEMON
Neikes
Gave me a purpose.

We wanted to get back at you
For what you've
Done to our families!

KREON
My family is by my side—

HAEMON
I'm talking about Eunice!

ANTIGONE & ISMENE
. . . Ma?!

HAEMON
She became a ghost,
Haunting the centre.
At times
She'd roar to the skies:

GET ME OUT OF HERE!
GET ME OUT!
GIVE ME MY HUSBAND'S EYES!
GIVE ME HIS TONGUE!
GIVE ME HIS LIFE!

KREON
WATCH YOUR—

HAEMON
She'd start chanting her children's names,
All through the night,
Wailing:
ANTIGONE
ISMENE
NEIKES
TEO.
I WANT TO SEE MY CHILDREN.
I BLAME KREON.
I BLAME MY HUSBAND.
I BLAME—

KREON
GUARD!

> ISMENE *is shaken,*
> *Trembling.*
> HAEMON *slips out of her grasp.*

HAEMON
KREON!

GUARD
OH SHUT IT.

> *The* GUARD *knocks* HAEMON *out.*
> *Silence.*

Pause.

KREON
Remove
Him.
But keep him alive
For further
Re-education.

The GUARD *does.*

ANTIGONE
What did you do,
Pa?

ISMENE
. . . Is it true?

KREON
Don't—
Don't believe that . . .
That BOY.
The weak spin tales to justify their crimes.

Beat.

Why were you with that traitor?
Why are you here?!
Have you both lost your minds?!

ANTIGONE
Ismene is lying.
She did nothing.
I did it all.

ISMENE
Uh . . .

ANTIGONE
I took Haemon in.
I helped him.
Ismene was simply a bystander.
She had no say in any of this.

ISMENE
No! I helped!
Don't blame Antigone, blame me too!

ANTIGONE
. . . Would you have come if I didn't run away?

ISMENE
. . .

ANTIGONE
You see, *Kreon*,
I came to the square alone.
She simply followed me out of her weak will.

ISMENE
Why must you be so cruel?

ANTIGONE
You'll thank me later.

KREON
I told you to stay home.
I warned you.
You know it's forbidden to be here!

ANTIGONE
Of course I know.

KREON
Yet you still came?!
Did I not make myself clear?
This is treason!
It is by LAW that I have to clear the square!

ANTIGONE
You call this law?
Some order sent by the Supreme Leader today becomes
A law you respect over your own family?

KREON
What are you talking about?

ANTIGONE
See for yourself.

> *ANTIGONE moves aside*
> *So that KREON can see his son.*
> *Beat.*

This is what your law has done for us.
And this is what you're wishing so hard
To clear from the square—
YOUR OWN SON.

KREON
HE IS NOT MY SON—

ANTIGONE
Your shame does not erase my brother from my blood!

> *Beat.*

We are surrounded by a field
Of wounded, dead, or lost.
With one word
You've chosen to brand them as *garbage*.
With the wave of a hand
You
Dismiss your son as waste!

If you clear this square
You will be dismissing all of us.
ALL OF US.

Stop this mess, Pa.
Stop it
Before it's too late!

KREON
I am your elder.
You MUST respect my words.
You MUST take my thoughts for law.

Sometimes . . .
We must start afresh,
By any means necessary.

And this.
This is a fresh start.
For our family.

ANTIGONE
I don't want *this* family of ghosts.
I'd rather be with them than stay here with you!

KREON
Don't be so selfish!

ANTIGONE
I'm not! Look around you!
All these people
Searching, calling, crying
For their missing families.
I'm speaking for them!
Don't erase us!

KREON
You're alone in thinking that's true.

ANTIGONE
No, we all think it.
You're just too blind to see it.

KREON
Have you no shame?

ANTIGONE
None at all
To reveal our family's shame for all to see.

KREON
Am I not your family too?

ANTIGONE
If you decide to hold the bulldozers, then yes,
You are still my pa.
If not, then you're a stranger to me.

KREON
Nothing is this black and white!

ANTIGONE
Nothing is black and white here!
We're surrounded by red!
RED!

KREON
Yes. A taint on our sacred square.
To be painted red by looting, hooting
Good-for-nothings.

ANTIGONE
No. Made red by the Supreme Leader—
NO—by YOUR pride.

    Beat.

Look at what's left of the square.
We have no power to stop you.
Only you can do that now.
Stop, Pa.

    Beat.

Be merciful.

KREON
You watch your tongue,
Or mercy will have no power to stop me.

ANTIGONE
You think you have power.
You think you're doing the right thing.
You've sacrificed your family
For reputation and honour,
For the Supreme Leader's pardon.

ANTIGONE: 方 | 211

That's not power.
That's stupidity.

KREON
Don't make me your enemy.

ANTIGONE
Too late.
I was born to love,
Yet I will end in hate.

KREON
Don't say that.
Don't break my heart.

ANTIGONE
Mine is already broken.

KREON
Please. Back down.

ANTIGONE
Please. Stop.

KREON
I can barely recognize my daughter anymore . . .
Ismene.
You are my witness.
You see how your sister rebels against me.
You see how she's broken the law.

    Beat.

(*to* ISMENE) Stand by me.
It's clear that Antigone stands alone in this.

ISMENE
Please, sister.
Don't do this—
Just say sorry!
Just let Pa do his job!

ANTIGONE
NO!
I must stand alone.
Save yourself,
Leave and live,
For the both of us.

KREON
Ismene. COME.
Antigone has chosen.
The tanks and bulldozers are close.
Let's see how long she stands.

ISMENE
Pa. We'll lose everything!

KREON
I'll still have you, as you'll still have me.

ISMENE
Will you harm your own daughter like this?

KREON
No harm in removing taint from our city.

ISMENE
You'll leave her here to die?

KREON
There's no time to waste.
The square must be cleared.

    Beat.

It's now or never, and look at her,
Still standing straight.
What arrogance.

ISMENE
So you're settled.

KREON
Don't waste your breath.
Stand by me
Or share in her fate.

                ISMENE does not know what to do.
        The sound of tanks and bulldozers inches closer.

ANTIGONE
Sister.
Live.
Do not forget me.
Spread tonight like wildfire.
Let it catch light and
Tell the world.
Tell the world about us.
About the square.
Don't let them forget.

                    ISMENE decides,
                Walks over to KREON,

Tears streaming down her face,
But she doesn't wince or make a sound.

KREON
Guard!

GUARD
Yessir.

KREON
Keep watch
Over her.
If she tries
Anything . . .

Then . . .

    Beat.

GUARD
Sir.
Are you asking me to—
To shoot your . . .

    Beat.

KREON
Keep watch.
That is all.

The GUARD *keeps a safe distance away,*
But stands vigilantly by ANTIGONE.

ANTIGONE *and* ISMENE *exchange a look.*

The clearing of the square
Begins.

                                    KREON and ISMENE turn away.

SCENE 14.

ANTIGONE looks like she's about to buckle at any second.

The bulldozers inch closer and closer.
The CHORUS begins to splinter from the square,
Fleeing for their lives:

CHORUS 1
Somebody help her!
Somebody, please!
Why are you all running from—

CHORUS 4
Oh, she's just one of them.
Listen to Kreon.
We need our peaceful square back.
Remove these rioters,
Send their bodies far away from
Our sacred SQUARE.

                        The sound of the bulldozers is at its peak.

                                Suddenly, from off stage

TIRESIA
STOP.

SCENE 15.

The world stops.

TIRESIA enters.
She hunches over a cane / umbrella.
She slowly moves her way to the centre,
Acknowledging ANTIGONE *as she passes her.*
It's as if the world (bulldozers included) moves aside for her
As she approaches KREON.

TIRESIA
Kreon.

Beat.

KREON
Headmistress.

KREON bows.

TIRESIA
May he will it.

KREON
Yes . . .
May he will it.

TIRESIA
I must speak to the square.

KREON
Yes.
Please
Remind our citizens here

Of HIS will,
Of HIS legacy,
And . . .
(privately with TIRESIA) Please.
Reason with Antigone.
She refuses to move.

TIRESIA
Your children have
A difficult relationship
With reason, just like you.

> *KREON hesitates but allows her to continue.*
> *KREON, the GUARD, and ISMENE stand a little*
> *Distance away as*
> *TIRESIA speaks to the square.*

Citizens.
I have served as your headmistress
For a decade now.
It has been my
Greatest

> *Beat.*

Regret.

> *Beat.*

I relinquish my position as headmistress—

KREON
Tiresia,
What are you doing?!
Guard,
Stop her!—

GUARD
Um,
Sir.

TIRESIA
(publicly) I have failed you all.
I abolish the re-education system.
I denounce its virtues.
I want nothing left to do with our
GLORIOUS Leader.
I cannot stand with him
In the face of this,
This mass burial.

The CHORUS murmurs.

KREON
(publicly) The clearing of the square is
For the greater good,
For the harmony of our city,
For the virtues passed down from our Leader.

This . . . old woman, is not to be trusted.
She's hysterical!
She—she holds revolutionary thoughts.
She clearly needs re-education!
Guard, stop her!—

TIRESIA
HEAR ME.
ALL OF YOU.
THIS IS KREON.
His wife Eunice and I created the centre.
Initially a sanctuary,
Twisted it into a prison

By you and-and that Supreme TYRANT
Against. OUR. WILL!

The CHORUS murmurs.

GUARD
Sir . . .
Is this true?!—

KREON
Don't listen to her!—

The GUARD doesn't move.
TIRESIA and KREON engage more privately.

TIRESIA
Kreon,
You are
Bending laws into unnatural omens,
Fighting opinions with weapons,
Wiping out the future of this CITY!

KREON
It was your duty to uphold the centre,
Yet you allowed this breach,
Leading us to this MESS.

   Beat.

I have done nothing wrong.
Our Supreme Leader has led us through
A thousand years of sweeping glory.

TIRESIA

You and I both know the truth about that little saying.
A thousand years? Really?
Come on now, don't—

KREON

The square must be cleared!

TIRESIA

No,
No,
Kreon,
If you clear the square,
The sun will curse this land,
And that cannot be undone.

The square is bloated with blood,
Sick from swelling with so many lost lives.
Do not let them be forgotten.

Heed my words.
Release Antigone.
Release the dead back
To their families.
Let them be buried in peace.
Or you will shatter
Laws older than you or me.

KREON

What laws?
I am following the law of the land!

TIRESIA

Have you forgotten,
The sacred belief
That white hair

Should never bury
Black hair?

Yet here you are, old man,
Burying a sea of black-haired seventeen-year-olds.

How do we make up for all this loss?
Where do we find the souls to fill that void?

You're right.
I am a part of this mess.
We both are, old friend.
We silenced a generation
In pursuit of harmony,
And for what?

When did we forget our humanity, Kreon?

I re-educated many of our friends.
They haunt me in my sleep.
Their remembrance must live on.

Years, YEARS
Down the line,
These memories will grow
In whispers and murmurs
Until one day
They rise and roar
And step on the false LAWS
We created.

They will read our names
And spit on our memory.

KREON
Guard!

> *The* GUARD *hesitates.*

LOCK HER UP.

GUARD
I-I—

KREON
Go!

> *The* GUARD *goes towards* TIRESIA.

GUARD
I'm . . . I'm sorry, ma'am . . .

TIRESIA
And
I'm sorry for all the friends you've lost tonight.

> TIRESIA *extends her arms.*
> *The* GUARD *takes her hands,*
> *Gently,*
> *Leaves her uncuffed.*
> *They begin to exit.*
> *Right before they fully go,*
> TIRESIA *turns to* KREON.

Kreon.
Do not let this be your greatest regret.
It's time for repentance, and release,
Not a further accumulation of shame.
Your son, Neikes,
Woke me up to that.
An unbending tree snaps at the sigh of a storm.
Yet
Storms heave and the grass simply shivers.

Do not be so unbending, Kreon.
You are bound to snap.

> *The GUARD takes TIRESIA to the rest of the CHORUS*
> *And leaves her with the group.*

KREON
Execute her.

> *ISMENE rushes to join.*

ISMENE
Pa.
I beg you.
Hear her words.

Look around you.

> *Everything is still.*

You have to stop this.

And . . .
Forgive Antigone. Please.
She's rash . . . but . . .
She's . . .

> *A long pause.*

KREON
(takes in a deep breath) CLEAR THE SQUARE.

ISMENE
NO!

GUARD
. . . Yessir!

> *ISMENE crumbles to the ground.*
> *ANTIGONE stands, defiant.*
> *The CHORUS stands, quivering.*
> *We hear the bulldozers starting up again.*
> *Closer and closer they step, one by one.*

CHORUS
This death-cast girl
Has become poetry
Escaping words.

ANTIGONE
Look.

CHORUS 1
Look.
Here they come.

ANTIGONE
. . . Off I go.

CHORUS 2
They're just leaving that girl there?!

ANTIGONE
. . . Off to catch that last gasp.

CHORUS 7
Leave her to her
Death wish.

ANTIGONE
. . . Off to be welcomed.

CHORUS 1
Help her!

ANTIGONE
I—

CHORUS 4
Somebody help her!

CHORUS 7
You do it.
I'm not joining her.

ANTIGONE
I am still alive.
I'll make my bed in the mud.

CHORUS (ALL)
Exactly.
Leave her.
Even Tiresia could not stop this.

CHORUS 1
Look!
Help her!

ANTIGONE
My youth raised up with the roaring flames.

CHORUS 7
Oh—

CHORUS 2
Oh my—

> **CHORUS 1**
> Oh my god—
> They're really going to—

ANTIGONE
What have I done?!

> **CHORUS 7**
> Help her!

> **CHORUS 2**
> Leave her!
> Save yourselves.

> **CHORUS 7**
> Nothing can be done.

> **CHORUS 4**
> Look.

> **CHORUS 5**
> Look.

> **CHORUS 1**
> LOOK.

ANTIGONE
I am—
I am undone!
The road is closing in on me.
The audience is watching, happy to be there,
Not here.
The end is steps,
Steps,
Steps,
Away.

Who will remember—
Neikes.
Ma.
Me?
Or the thousands of us here.
Who will remember us?

I will scream it to the skies:
On June fourth,
Tanks ripped through the mountains,
Convulsed the seas, and
Flowers bloomed in one lonely colour.
We were made to be forgotten.
But never forget.

I was caught
In a web of
Unyielding yearning.

CHORUS
Amazing
How
Forgetting
Birth's violent remembrance,
How
The fallen
Nourish
The standing
Until they too
Fall.

We all turn away from the sight.
We cannot see it happen,
Or even hear it.

> ANTIGONE *goes with the river of umbrellas.*
> *Everyone is still.*

SCENE 16.

ISMENE
What have you done?

KREON
. . .

> ISMENE *grabs* KREON.

ISMENE
What have you done?

> ISMENE *slaps her pa.*

You had a family,
A wife,
Four children,
And now . . . now
It's just you and me.

> *Beat.*

You ruined us.

And not just our family.
All these people
Will never be able
To find their dead.

KREON
I did this for our nation,
For the Supreme Leader,
This had to be done—

ISMENE
Everything is a choice, Pa.
I will never forgive you.

KREON
Don't say that, Ismene.

ISMENE
You are entirely alone now, *Kreon.*

> *Suddenly,* ISMENE *rushes out to find* ANTIGONE's *body.*

GUARD
MISSY!
COME BACK HERE.

KREON
ISMENE, STAY WITH ME.

GUARD
Sir?!
Should I shoot her—

KREON
(to himself) No.

GUARD
She's in the way!
Sir—if I don't get her,
The bulldozers will.

KREON
(to himself) . . . No . . .

GUARD
Sir?!
What should I do?

> *ISMENE discovers her sister's body.*
> *She holds ANTIGONE and wails.*

ISMENE
AHHHHHHHHHHHHHHHHHHHHHHHHHHHHHHH!

GUARD
Sir!
What do I do?!

> *The bulldozers are close.*

SIR!?

KREON
(slowly whispers) . . . Stop.
(orders) Stop the tanks!
Stop the bulldozers!

GUARD
WHAT?! Really?!

> **CHORUS**
> Did we hear correctly?

KREON
Stop clearing the square!

GUARD
(to the other guards) Stop! Stop!

CHORUS
He said stop!

KREON
Stop this chaos!

CHORUS
Stop!
Kreon just ordered it:
Stop!

KREON
Guard.
Go help the citizens
Retrieve their dead.
GO.

GUARD
Yessir.

KREON
Rummages through the field of umbrellas
To join ISMENE, ANTIGONE, *and* NEIKES.

CHORUS
Stop. Stop. Stop.
Quickly,
Spread the word.
Quickly.
Let it thunder through the streets.
The square, the square, the square
Is free!

Come claim your families,
Come help your friends,
Come honour your fallen.

The fangs of the beast
Have shut in mercy.

CHORUS 2
But what about tomorrow?

CHORUS 4
Who knows . . .

CHORUS 5
What will the Supreme Leader do?

CHORUS 4
Who knows . . .

CHORUS 5
What about us?
What about the city?
What happened to that Haemon?

CHORUS 1
He'll be sent back for re-education.

CHORUS 5
To be forgotten again?
What good will that do?

CHORUS 4
Who knows?

CHORUS 5
What happens after?

CHORUS 4
Only tomorrow will tell.

> *Beat.*

Is that . . .

CHORUS 2
That's Kreon with his daughters and son.

CHORUS 7
Ismene with her brother and sister.

> *Beat.*

May that family
Rest in peace.

CHORUS 2
Live in peace, too.

CHORUS 1
I do not wish them well.
I can't.

CHORUS 7
. . . I understand.

> *KREON and ISMENE are clutching two umbrellas.*
> *We cannot hear them.*
> *As they ritually cover, respect, and honour their kin,*
> *The CHORUS stand in a moon around ANTIGONE.*
> *ANTIGONE's body rests.*

CHORUS

Antigone,

Your pa,

Who holds you now,

His world was shattered under a red and golden flag.

Your pa,

Your own blood,

He was far too late

To see

How you are

Seventeen already, forever.

It rains for you, Antigone.

Though

Is it rain or drifting ash?

Let wisdom guide our tomorrow.

Let remembrance carve its place.

Let great men hold their great words

And listen,

Truly listen:

For the forgotten do not forget.

They swell back to life generation after generation.

Like that dim light just before the dawn.

The fallen umbrellas begin to tremble

As they rise and rise and rise into the air

And the sun is restored.

END.

ACKNOWLEDGEMENTS

These plays were written on the traditional territory of the Mississaugas of the Credit, the Anishinaabeg, the Chippewa, the Haudenosaunee, and the Wendat peoples.

My endless gratitude for every single collaborator that brought these two plays to life: to Young People's Theatre (Stephen and Karen) and Saga Collectif (Jonathan) for these initial commissions, and for the gift of diving into adaptations, a path that has changed my life; to every single artist and ally that has contributed to various stages of each play's life—you are countless, beautiful, talented souls that have forever become embedded into the DNA of these plays; to Ian for guiding my path; to Pierre for endless love and support; to the blessing that is dramaturgs, Stephen, Brian, Joanna, Karen, and Charlotte, thank you for being champions; and to all those in history that have fought to remember the events and histories that shape humanity—I will never forget you.

Thank you as well to YPT, Saga Collectif, Theatre Passe Muraille, Tarragon Theatre, the Stratford Festival, Cahoots Theatre, Factory Theatre, the Ontario Arts Council, the Canada Council for the Arts, and the Toronto Arts Council for your support of these works.

Ho Ka Kei / Jeff Ho is a Toronto-based theatre artist, originally from Hong Kong. His works include *Iphigenia and the Furies (On Taurian Land)*, *Antigone: 方*, and *trace*. His work has been developed by the Stratford Festival, Tarragon Theatre, Young People's Theatre, Human Cargo, Factory Theatre, Cahoots Theatre, the Banff Playwrights Lab, and Nightswimming Theatre. Jeff is grateful to have been honoured with a Toronto Theatre Critics Award for Best New Canadian Play (*Iphigenia*), the Jon Kaplan Legacy Fund Award for a Young Canadian Playwright, the Bulmash-Siegel New Creation Development Award (Tarragon Theatre), four Dora Mavor Moore Award nominations, and a Harold Award (House of Nadia Ross). He is a graduate of the National Theatre School.

First edition: March 2022
Printed and bound in Canada by Imprimerie Gauvin, Gatineau

Jacket art by Jeremy Leung
Author photo © Dahlia Katz

**PLAYWRIGHTS
CANADA PRESS**

202-269 Richmond St. w.
Toronto, ON
M5V 1X1

416.703.0013
info@playwrightscanada.com
www.playwrightscanada.com
@playcanpress